Crypto Trading Success

2022

**Step by Step Guide for Beginners
Invest profitably in Bitcoin and Ethereum**

About This Guide

This is an educational guide to trading cryptocurrencies. It was written by a group of traders who have survived a series of peaks and troughs during 10 years in the crypto market, making life-changing profits in the process.

We would like to show you what we believe are the most effective strategies you can use to profit from these markets, without too much pain or anxiety.

The fact is that cryptocurrencies are extremely volatile. You do need to be clear about what you are doing or you'll make terrible mistakes. With that in mind, please do heed the warning in the disclaimer that starts and closes this book. Cryptocurrencies do carry very significant risk and you have to be prepared to lose some or all of your investment. If you are in any doubt please do seek independent financial advice.

The good news is that you don't need any special equipment or excessive training. And what you'll find is that it's possible to earn serious profits in these markets without too much time input.

Table of Contents

Introduction:

3 Ways to Make Money in Crypto

Chapter 1

The First Question That Everyone Asks

Chapter 2

Buying Cryptocurrencies

Chapter 3

The Simplest Way to Make Money in Crypto

Chapter 4

Trading the Cycle

Chapter 5

Staking

Chapter 6

AirDrops

Chapter 7

The Growth Mindset

Chapter 8

Your Next Steps

Introduction:
3 Ways to Make Money in Crypto

On 3rd January, 2009, a new technology was launched in an obscure Internet forum. It was called Bitcoin. And according to its anonymous designer, it promised a new type of money, one that could float free of the existing financial system.

There was no need for a bank or an authority to control this new money. Anybody with a smartphone could buy Bitcoin and send it to anyone else. There was no need for credit checks or passports or a bank. Perfect strangers could send each other money without knowing anything about each other.

It took a while for this revolutionary idea to take hold. The first purchase was recorded in May 2010 – two large Papa John's pizzas worth $30 were bought with 10,000 Bitcoins. In those early days, cryptocurrencies were the domain of cryptographers, computer scientists and criminals.

But from 2009 to July 2011, Bitcoin rose in value from $1 to $30. That got the attention of Silicon Valley.

And then from April 2013 to December 2013, there was a second huge bull run, with Bitcoin running from $250 to $1,100, causing a stampede of investors who were willing to go through risky channels to buy the currency. The main source of liquidity in the market those days was Mt Gox, an exchange listed in Japan. When that collapsed under a devastating hack the price of Bitcoin collapsed: falling 80% from peak to trough.

The media claimed the dream was 'over'. Obituaries were written. The idea that Bitcoin could disturb, destroy or replace the traditional banking system seemed ridiculous. The price bounced along a narrow range for a year and scores of investors lost faith and quit the markets.

Then… as the likes of big banks and tech companies took an interest in crypto, it began to climb again, attracting a huge population of new investors eager to participate in rampant speculation.

And this pattern keeps repeating again and again.

As we write this book, Bitcoin has run through *multiple* cycles in which it has grown exponentially then fallen 70 - 80% in the correction that follows. Investors get excited. People make fortunes. Then they get burned out during the bear market.

Today, Bitcoin is used by millions around the globe as a store of value: a way to protect their money from economic problems in their home country. The technology has been so impressive that everyone from the Bank of England to Kim Kardashian is rushing to develop a version of their own.

But cryptocurrencies are also crazily volatile. You have never seen a more volatile asset class than cryptocurrencies. As a crypto trader, you can sometimes go through long months of tedium where you sit on your hands, just waiting for something to happen.

And then suddenly the market lights up. Coins start jumping 200% or 300%. The whole thing takes on a new thrilling momentum. But even as it travels towards new all-time highs, the price of Bitcoin still drops, and recovers, rolls and rights itself. Sometimes it drops 50% in a matter of days.

It can be too much for some people. The number one reason why people quit crypto is that they can't handle their emotions when it comes to these markets (we'll talk a lot about trading and emotions later in this book).

A lot of new traders quit after their first big crash in the market even if they've made money overall. They lose their appetite for risk. They feel stupid. Maybe they bought the wrong coin and got depressed when it crashed 90%. Or maybe they soldier on till the next bullish phase but get exhausted by the constant ups and downs in the market.

But it doesn't have to be that way.

The Buy and Hold Method

In this guide we are going to show you some very simple ways to make money from crypto.

We'll start by addressing the most frequent questions we get asked by new traders (Chapter 1). In Chapter 2, we show you how you can buy crypto.

Then we'll start on the good stuff: how to start making money trading crypto.

When most new investors get involved in crypto, they buy Bitcoin and just sit on it. And that's fine. This 'buy and hold' strategy is a proven way to make money. We believe that Bitcoin and many other cryptos will still be here in 10 years, and if you buy now, you could make a very serious return.

In Chapter 3, we will explain why, in our experience, buying and holding cryptocurrencies for the long term is the single best way to make money in this market. It removes the stress and it prevents you from making mistakes when you trade.

In fact, some of the most sophisticated traders we know have decided that the best way to make money in crypto is to step back from the screen entirely.

But if that's all you're doing, you are missing out.

There are many other ways that expert investors and traders make money from crypto. These methods can help you build a healthy income stream and benefit from huge pay-outs, all without having to stomach the wild volatility.

The Staking Method

Take staking, which we cover in Chapter 5. This is a relatively new phenomenon in crypto and it is proving to be enormously popular. The idea is that you invest in a cryptocurrency and then lend it back to the network. In exchange, you receive a very healthy stream of income. From 4 - 6% APR on some of the bellwether coins, to 120% APR or more on some of the high-risk coins.

It's been a revelation for a lot of crypto traders. Instead of looking at the screen all day, you invest in the cryptocurrency that you have most faith in, something you would be prepared to hold for months or years, and then stake and forget about it. If you want to release your funds, you can simply un-stake and your coins will be returned (after a cooling off period), along with the rewards and interest that you've earned.

It's not quite as safe as keeping your money in a bank, where your capital is covered by deposit insurance and capital compensation schemes but the rewards for staking crypto are very attractive.

On some of the more popular crypto exchanges, you can stake a wide variety of coins and earn an annualised yield of 6%, 15%… even 30%+ in just a couple of clicks.

In this book, we'll give you a comprehensive review of the best ways to stake your coins and the best places to stake. The rewards. The risks. This will help you develop a basic staking strategy, so you can earn a decent return on coins, no matter what stage you are at in the cycle.

The AirDrop Method

AirDrops are another of the hottest opportunities right now in the crypto space. It's a way to make thousands (even tens of thousands) of pounds from free 'gifted' cryptos.

In this book, you'll discover everything you need to know about AirDrops: what they are, the pros, the cons, the caveats and the best strategies.

We've successfully received three and even four-figure gains from single AirDrops in the past, so this is definitely worth your attention.

A little bit of effort and luck is needed and AirDrop hunting won't be for everyone. However, if you have the time and the patience it can be a great way to make substantial extra gains from your crypto investing.

Getting Started

As you'll see, it's very easy to get started.

If you have a computer and a mobile phone you have everything you need. You don't need any previous experience or special skills.

The number one thing we always say to everyone involved in this is… it's about keeping it simple and staying the course.

Let's start by addressing some of the most frequently asked questions about cryptocurrencies.

Chapter 1

The First Question That Everyone Asks

We'll start with some good news: compared to the early days in this market, buying and trading cryptos is actually very easy. In fact, once you are set up, it only takes a few clicks. In the next chapter, we will show you how to get set up, what to buy, and when to buy.

We'll talk through the experience of some of the most successful traders in our group: from newbies who turned £12k into £116,000 in their first year, to more sophisticated traders who have quit their jobs to focus on crypto full-time.

But no matter what level you are at, people always have the same questions when they first start out in crypto. We have compiled a comprehensive list over the years so let's start there.

Q: How can I make money from Bitcoin or cryptos?

A: You can buy and hold cryptos (such as Bitcoin) just like you can any asset such as shares, property or gold. If the value goes up over time you can sell it back into pounds, dollars or euros for a profit.

You can also trade them for other cryptos (more on this later) and again the principles are the same. If you buy low and sell high you make a profit. Advanced traders can make money from Bitcoin in falling markets too by 'shorting' it (making a prediction the price will go down) like you can with spread betting.

Q: Who created Bitcoin?

A: Bitcoin was invented on the 31st October 2008 by Satoshi Nakamoto and then released as open-source software in 2009.

It has an in-built system of checks and balances that means it's at all times audited and provable by anyone who cares to look. This means it cannot be corrupted in the same way that 'traditional' currencies can.

Satoshi's anonymity often raises unjustified concerns because of a misunderstanding of Bitcoin's open-source nature. Satoshi has no way of undermining the system – it is entirely independent of him – and indeed everyone has access to all of the source code all of the time.

The Bitcoin system is peer-to-peer and because of this no one person or group controls it or can manipulate it. That means any developer can review or modify the software code and indeed the original code has been adapted and improved over the years. So, in this sense the identity of Bitcoin's creator is about as relevant today as the identity of the person who invented paper.

Q: How does Bitcoin work?

A: Bitcoin is a 'digital' currency. You can send it from one person to another or use it to buy goods and services. From a technical perspective, the blockchain (the technology which powers Bitcoin) is the brains behind it.

The blockchain records every single Bitcoin transaction – past and present – and the ownership of every Bitcoin in circulation. Once again, this record (often referred to as a decentralised ledger) cannot be forged or manipulated by individuals, groups or even governments.

This is one of the reasons that Bitcoin is so popular. Technology-wise it's a bit like upgrading from snail mail to email.

Q: Do I trade cryptos or do I actually own them?

A: You actually own them*. You can exchange them for different cryptocurrencies, if you want to, and of course you can sell them back into currency (pounds, dollars, euros etc.). More on this in a moment.

* Some companies now offer the opportunity to buy options on them, but we suggest that until you are very familiar with cryptocurrency trading you stick to the traditional investing style.

Q: It looks very expensive; do I have to buy a whole Bitcoin?

A: Absolutely not. Otherwise you'd have to stump up thousands for a single Bitcoin each time, which would make it out of reach for most.

Think of Bitcoins in decimals. You can buy 0.1 of a Bitcoin if you want to, or 0.5 and so on. In the exchanges where you buy Bitcoin you can simply enter the sum you want to spend on them, e.g. £100, and it'll work it out for you.

Q: How do I access my funds? Is it real money?

A: Yes! It's absolutely real money. If you want to sell any of your coins back into currency it's just a case of following a few simple steps and the money is transferred into your bank account.

You can do this any time you want. Most exchanges say it can take a few days to clear but typically it's less than 24 hours.

Q: How do I buy Bitcoin and other cryptos?

A: The most common place to get hold of Bitcoin and other cryptos is on one of the online cryptocurrency exchanges. These are websites where you can exchange your money (pounds, dollars, euros) for crypto.

In return the exchange takes a small commission. There are also some offline vendors as well where you can buy and sell Bitcoin and even a growing number of Bitcoin ATMs.

Three reputable online exchanges where you can buy and sell crypto on in the UK and Europe are Coinbase, Kraken and Bitstamp (Important Note: we are not acting as an affiliate to any of these exchanges but mention them purely because they are the ones our team use. You'll find more information about our favourite exchanges in the Resource Guide at

Q: How is Bitcoin priced?

A: Bitcoin is like any other currency in that its value can go up and down relative to other currencies.

As there are only a fixed number of Bitcoins that can ever be in circulation (the total number of Bitcoin is capped at 21 million) it's not subject to inflation in the same way that state or national currencies are. You can't just print off more Bitcoin.

So the price is entirely dependent on supply and demand. If 10 million people are all trying to buy Bitcoin at the same time, the price will rocket and vice versa.

Q: What's the difference between Bitcoin and other cryptos or cryptocurrencies?

A: Bitcoin is the original and by far the most widely-used and accepted cryptocurrency. So why do these alternative cryptocurrencies even exist?

Well, like Bitcoin, they also offer a way to pay for things or to transfer money from person A to person B. Where they differ slightly is in how they use the technology.

Some claim to be completely untraceable to governments or individuals (Bitcoin, with a lot of effort can be traced). This makes them appealing to people who want total anonymity.

Others claim they are faster or require less energy to run. The Bitcoin network uses quite a lot of electricity when you tally up the whole enterprise.

So there are some differences between them and each has its own target users. You then also have non-currency-based cryptos. You may have heard of coins like Ethereum.

This is a crypto platform where developers can build services powered by its own coin, Ether.

So when you invest in Ether, you're effectively investing in the company or the idea and how scalable it is – a bit like if you were to invest in stocks or shares.

Simply put:

Coins like Bitcoin = cryptocurrency

Coins like Ethereum = platforms that use cryptocurrency (or blockchain) technology

Q: What are the advantages of using Bitcoin?

A1. Long term, it's considered a better store of value than 'traditional' currency.

Bitcoin cannot be manipulated, counterfeited or otherwise meddled with by governments, corporations or any one individual.

This might not sound like a big deal but this is really important.

Governments can, and do, regularly manipulate national currencies to suit their own ends.

In Argentina, a country recently beset by bad debt and economic mismanagement, inflation hit 40% in 2016.

In Venezuela, a once prosperous economy bursting with oil and natural resources, inflation recently hit 248.6%!

And in Zimbabwe the government printed so much money to cling onto power that inflation reached 79.6 billion per cent in 2015.

These are not isolated cases.

Even in developed countries, inflation can be high and it can compound over many years, devaluing national currencies.

In countries where there is high inflation but good Internet access, Bitcoin is extremely prevalent and it's easy to see why.

Bitcoin is a secure and valid store of wealth and method of payment for people in uncertain economic environments.

After all, why put your trust and hard-earned money into the national currency when it could be worth half as much in a year's time as it is today?

While we might feel immune from this kind of economic mismanagement in countries like the UK and USA we are still at the mercy of government policy. Regardless, if there's a change of government, a war, a regime change, Bitcoin cannot be meddled with.

A2. It's popular with individuals who don't want their activity traced.

Bitcoin is popular with libertarians who don't think that governments and individuals should be able to control and manipulate wealth.

They want an alternative model that puts freedom in the hands of people not governments.

It has also found a fanbase among some darker regions of the Internet and is often used by criminals to buy and sell drugs online because, like cash in the offline world, it is harder to trace. (However, Bitcoin itself is not completely untraceable and unless users go through some effort to cover their tracks it often can be linked back to an individual. With that said, there are alternative cryptocurrencies which cannot be tracked).

A3. It's a more advanced way to deal with financial transactions and doesn't require middlemen.

When you make transactions using traditional currency you need all sorts of complicated, often manual, checks and balances in place as well as intermediaries… a bank, a clearing house, all the associated staff and, of course, all the regulators, including the government.

Bitcoin dispenses with a lot of that while providing a more secure and transparent system with which to make transactions.

Q: Who uses Bitcoin?

1. Ordinary people who want to use a currency that isn't held and controlled by banks and governments.
2. People in countries that are suffering from economic problems (whether that's hyperinflation, government corruption or strict controls) and want a safer space to store their wealth and a trustworthy way to transfer money to friends and family both domestically and internationally.
3. Investors who can see the rapid adoption of this exciting new technology and currency as inevitable and want to profit from its increasing value.
4. The biggest proven use of blockchain so far is money. Bitcoin has become a substitute for gold in many countries. And the cryptocurrencies that followed in its wake are disrupting many of the traditional pillars of the financial system: lending, securities, derivatives, exchanges. Billions of pounds and dollars have migrated to this new system in the last year. And there are huge potential gains for early investors.

Q: How are Bitcoins created?

A: There are 21 million Bitcoins in total although not all of them are in circulation yet. The remainder have to be brought to the surface in a process called 'mining'.

Think of it like gold. There's only a fixed amount of gold on our planet. It's there for the taking, but it needs to be mined (we'll cover what 'mining' for Bitcoin involves later!). It's the same with Bitcoin. Current estimates are that this won't be completed until around the year 2140. Even after the very last Bitcoin has been mined, miners will still be incentivised to keep confirming transactions.

Q: Is it risky to invest or trade in Bitcoin/cryptos?

A: It can be, but there are ways to reduce that risk significantly.

While the markets can be very volatile, at the Crypto Traders' Academy, we firmly believe cryptos are here to stay.

The useful ones that find a place in our day-to-day lives will continue to go up in value.

From an investor's point of view they are extremely volatile and coins can go up 2,000%, 3,000%, 5,000% in a matter of weeks or months. By the same token they can also crash hard.

You do need to have a strong stomach. Wild gains can easily be followed by devastating losses. It's important to only put in what you can potentially afford to lose in the short term. If you are prepared to wait for the long term, the potential returns could be extraordinary.

What Next…

We hope that's given you a taster. If you're new to this world we understand it can feel a little scary and strange.

There's so much hype and nonsense written about this subject that our mission is to cut through all that. Most of it's written by people who don't have a clue what they're talking about.

This misinformation makes us angry because it's dangerous and could lose you money. So, our aim at Crypto Traders' Academy is to guide you on the right path and give you the right tools and mindset for trading the crypto markets profitably.

If you're careful, and you follow a few basic rules, then this really could be the most incredible opportunity to make money that many of us will ever encounter in our lifetimes.

We can't emphasise that strongly enough.

As one of our lead traders, Michael, always says, "If we have another year like 2017" – and he strongly believes that we will – then "we may never have to work again."

His analysis of the six major cycles so far is that there is an average upside of 6,000% from peak to trough. So, the opportunity here is outrageous, really.

That's why we've created this book.

Your next step: Get some skin in the game and buy some Bitcoin.

Chapter 2

Buying Cryptocurrencies

The first thing you need to do is get yourself registered on an exchange. Exchanges are online marketplaces where you can buy and trade cryptocurrencies. They're a bit like a bureau de change, but for cryptos. We have a few that we favour, including Coinbase and Kraken. In a moment, we'll run through the ins and outs of using these platforms.

Before You Get Cracking, a Quick Heads-Up…

Getting registered on the exchanges can be frustrating at times. We don't want to sugar-coat it. This is probably the hardest part for most people and while it's not a difficult process there can sometimes be delays.

The crypto market has matured since we started. And it's a lot easier to get involved these days. The exchanges are more user-friendly. But still you might experience a few small obstacles that require your patience.

For example, you often have to take a picture of your passport to get through the security checks, and this can be a bit of a faff. And because of the unprecedented demand for cryptos right now, the influx of new users is huge. This means many exchanges are experiencing processing delays.

The thing to remember is that you only ever have to register for each exchange once (when it's done it's done!).

The buying and selling part is then very straightforward.

Please be patient because it really is worth it in the end. If one exchange isn't taking on members, there are plenty of others we can recommend in the meantime.

Some approvals will go through in a few hours, others can take a few days.

To find out the latest information on crypto exchanges, head over to our free Resource Guide.

You can access it here:

http://thecta.io/resourceguide

Your First Exchange: Kraken

If you want to make a start with crypto, the best way is to get set up on Kraken. This exchange will allow you to buy Bitcoin, Ethereum and a host of other coins.

Kraken is one of the most reputable, long standing exchanges and is also one of the easiest to use. They also have a mobile app which allows you to buy, sell, and react to price alerts on your favourite coins from your phone.

There is good liquidity on the exchange and it's easy to transfer money in and out of your bank account.

In terms of fees, Kraken also offer good value compared to some of its competitors.

Kraken Exchange Guide

About Kraken:

One of the most reputable, long standing exchanges in the crypto space and a favourite at CTA.

Pros: Very low fees, user friendly guides, excellent security
Cons: Less obvious user interface at first
Security: View their security protocols and proof of audit

Quick Summary:

- Founded in 2011 by Jesse Powell
- Headquarters in San Francisco
- Over 6 million clients in 190 countries
- Does nearly $1 billion a day trade volume
- It is owned by Paward Inc

For a step-by-step guide on how to set up a new account on Kraken so that you can start using the platform, visit here: https://support.kraken.com/hc/en-us/articles/226090548

Get Set Up on Other Exchanges as Soon as You Can

So your first step is to set aside time to get set up on Kraken.

And if you have trouble making transactions on Kraken, or you get frustrated with the approval process, don't despair.

There are several other very user-friendly exchanges, e.g. Coinbase. We use all of these exchanges ourselves. In fact, it's worth setting up a number of crypto exchanges when you have the chance. Some coins on Coinbase are not available on Kraken for example.

As with anything worth having, you just have to get through this first stage and then it starts getting a lot easier. Once you've got this out of the way... the real fun begins.

Here's some information about Coinbase:

Coinbase Exchange Guide

About Coinbase:

Coinbase is one of the best known crypto exchanges and has a pared down, easy to use interface.

Pros: Very reputable exchange, user friendly, strong security
Cons: Smaller coin selection, slightly higher trading fees
Security Measures: View Coinbase's insurance policy here

Quick Summary:

- *Launched in 2012 by Brian Armstrong and Fred Ehrsam*
- *Offices in New York, London, Dublin, Tokyo and more*
- *Over 73 million verified users*
- *Went public on the Nasdaq on April 14, 2021*
- *Valued at $48 billion in January 2022*

How to set up a new account on Coinbase
https://help.coinbase.com/en/coinbase/getting-started/getting-started-with-coinbase/create-a-coinbase-account

The two exchanges we've just discussed (particularly Kraken) are two that our experts (and Crypto Traders' Academy members) trade with on a regular basis.

They have strong liquidity, robust security measures in place, and are easy to use and accessible, particularly if you are UK or Europe-based. We have no affiliation with and receive no kickbacks from any of the exchanges listed.

Tips on Using Exchanges

First time depositing money to a crypto exchange? Check you are using a crypto-friendly bank first. Some banks are crypto-friendly but some aren't and will block transactions and generally cause a headache. You can save yourself a huge amount of time by checking first and only using crypto-friendly banks to deposit or withdraw. Take a look at your bank's crypto policy online, or simply contact them directly, and they should be able to advise you.

First time sending crypto between wallets or exchanges? Send a small test amount first. If you're sending large amounts it's often worth doing a separate test first (worth a few £) to check you have the address set up correctly. You can then send as much as you want on subsequent transfers.

When you deposit cash from your bank account always choose odd numbers (not rounded ones). Depositing large, round cash sums can sometimes trigger extra bank checks and delay deposits or withdrawals. To mitigate delays try to deposit specific amounts instead, e.g. £976.99 instead of £1,000.

UK-based? Depositing or withdrawing cash using the 'FPS' option is almost always the best option. FPS (or 'Faster Payments Service') deposits and withdrawals are usually almost instant (unless the bank flags it, which does happen!) and they're also the cheapest. Typically, they are only a couple of pounds or free.

Chapter 3

The Simplest Way to Make Money in Crypto

Now that you are set up, the next step is to start buying coins.

Bitcoin is the first starting point for most traders. It's the bellwether. All coins in crypto tend to follow Bitcoin's lead first and foremost. When it pumps, others follow.

There are several long-term catalysts for Bitcoin.

Monetary stimulus: Money printing by central banks drives investors towards Bitcoin, which like an improved version of gold, prefers easier monetary conditions. Unlike gold, Bitcoin thrives in a 'risk on' environment.

Institutional interest: A regulated cryptocurrency market is attractive to institutional investors. There is huge pent-up demand from clients. The market offers outsized returns. And crypto returns are often uncorrelated with most other assets. Institutional money is a huge catalyst for cryptocurrencies.

Inheritance windfall: Millennial investors will inherit an estimated $10 trillion over the next 10 years. We could see a huge transfer of wealth into cryptocurrencies from this cohort.

Tech invasion: Financial institutions realise that blockchain is a technology that could radically improve their systems, potentially staving off an invasion of tech giants, such as Alibaba, Amazon and Google, who are already moving quickly into online payments and banking. Microsoft and Facebook have announced crypto projects of their own. Blockchain could be the bedrock of a new system that significantly reduces friction (unnecessary fees, call centres, delays, privacy breaches, and generally antiquated processes) and provides a more modern user experience.

New ways of interacting with each other: Crypto and particularly Ethereum-based apps could reinvent huge aspects of our day-to-day lives: from how individuals and companies transact with each other to how our identities are verified. One thing we know for sure is that with blockchain the basic technology is already there and the pace of innovation is breathtaking.

Ultimately, Bitcoin is a speculation on what could be a safe haven for millions, a new payment system and a hedge against long-term inflation of fiat currencies like USD, EUR or GBP. In the near future, if Bitcoin were to take just 25% of gold's market cap, it would scale towards a market cap of $2.5 trillion and a price per Bitcoin of $150,000.

The key risk with Bitcoin, as with most crypto, is regulation from global governments. Just like the Internet, this risk decreases each year it exists as governments become more familiar with it.

But if you want to make money in crypto, then our team believe that holding Bitcoin is a must. It's far less volatile than some of the other coins. Having a decent allocation to Bitcoin will help you through some of the wilder swings in the market.

The Beauty of Buy and Hold

How much Bitcoin should you buy?

Well, that's a question of personal choice. It will depend on your appetite for risk. If you are just starting out, a sensible approach is to have a 20% to 30% allocation to Bitcoin. And another 30% allocation to Ethereum (more on that coin in a moment).

Remember again: these are highly volatile assets and even if you are buying a bellwether coin such as Bitcoin, you are still exposed to heavy volatility and wild swings in the price.

But if you want to keep things simple, you could buy Bitcoin and just sit on it.

The beauty of buying and holding is that you don't have to suffer through the chaos in the market. You can read about the fundamentals behind the story. How it works. Why it's trusted. Why the likes of Goldman Sachs and Fidelity are rushing to buy this particular cryptocurrency.

You can read about the risks. The volatility. And once you get comfortable with the investment case, you might decide that the best thing to do is to simply buy a stack and forget about it. Wait for Bitcoin to climb and fall and climb and fall, safe in the knowledge that the long-term trend is up.

In our experience, the biggest profits are typically made by accumulating fundamentally solid coins at low prices and holding long term and making a minimum amount of trades.

In fact, one of the quickest ways to lose money is to trade too much.

Terrance Odean, a professor at the University of California, Berkeley, has spent most of his career studying these mistakes. He has particular interest in the traits and sins that lead us to make irrational decisions when we trade. His work is full of the stupidity, overconfidence, short sightedness, and a seemingly hard-wired tendency to follow the herd into popular investments.

But one conclusion runs through his work from the start – the worst trait you can have is to be too active a trader.

In 1999, Odean published a study in which he followed the investments of 10,000 brokerage accounts over a year. He wanted to investigate just how much skill it took to trade stocks successfully.

The results were sobering.

"On average, the shares that individual traders sold did better than those they bought by a substantial margin – 3.2 percentage points per year, above and beyond the costs of executing the trades."

In a paper entitled 'Trading is Hazardous to Your Wealth', Odean and his colleague Brad Barber found that on average, it was the most active traders who had the poorest returns, while the most passive who performed best.

The reality is that if you trade less, you save on transaction fees, but you also stop yourself from making silly mistakes.

Buying at the wrong time. Selling your losers. Not running your winners.

One of the original founders in our group, Finn, bought his first Bitcoin in 2011.

His investment of £1,500 is worth millions today.

OK, he was very early. But his approach hasn't really changed over the years. He does a huge amount of research to find the coins with the most potential. And then he sits on those coins for years, barely troubled by the swings in the market. He doesn't seem to have aged at all in the last 10 years!

And we see this approach pay off all the time.

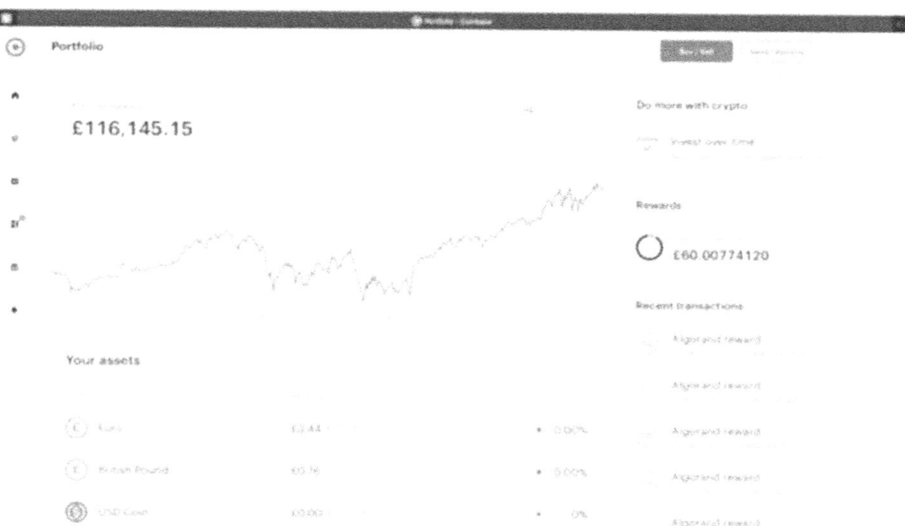

One of the more successful traders in the Crypto Traders' Academy recently, W.G, bought a handful of coins in 2019 and sat on them until they had exploded in price.

"I had £12K, at the start," says W.G. "It topped out at over £160K and I'm very confident that that number will be much bigger in the months to come."

We share his confidence in the long-term approach.

If you then take that number and compound it through further cycles over the next decade, you really could make life-changing returns from this.

What coins might be worth holding for that long?

Well, there are plenty of options. But if you really want to keep it simple, you should just start by investing in Ethereum.

Buy Ethereum

This is by far our favourite cryptocurrency. Most of us in the Crypto Traders' Academy have at least 30% or more of our crypto portfolio in Ethereum.

This platform, built by a ragtag group of feuding hackers in a remote Swiss village, has managed to pioneer a whole new way of organising society.

Today it's on its way to being a trillion-dollar system, with people lending, borrowing, trading, voting, governing… and every other kind of human activity you could imagine.

We at the Crypto Traders' Academy think that Ethereum has the potential to scale massively from here, with the price of Ethereum, the native currency on this platform, rising to $9,000-$15,000 over this cycle and more afterwards.

We believe the Ethereum platform, and the apps that sit on it, have the potential to create an economy with a GDP larger than the USA today.

If Ethereum scales as we expect, then it's likely that a host of the other projects that are pitching up on the Ethereum platform could deliver 10 times, 20 times, perhaps even 50 times your investment for the really high-risk projects. Let's take a deep dive into the story, just to explain why we are so bullish about this coin.

Welcome to Nomadland

Let's say you decide to start over.

You pack up your belongings in a car and you take your family and head out into the wilderness.

What will you need to make life work? Well, you will need land. After six hours of driving, you find a valley with running water, good roads and fresh pasture.

You will need housing and basic utilities. Thankfully, the sun shines for most of the year in these parts, and with a background in engineering, you rig up a few solar panels to manage the energy needs of your family.

Six months in, news of your settlement starts to reach local media. And people are inspired. By the time that news reaches the national press, there are copycat projects set in patches of free land all around the country. Your little settlement now has a community of 1,000 people. And you start to trade with each other. First, labour and money. Then tools and energy from the panels. And then you start trading with other settlements, forming a decentralised economy of strangers that operates on its own rules and agreements.

Introducing Ether…

One day, after weeks of new arrivals to the camp, you decide to develop your own currency. You call it 'Ether'. And the next morning, you decide to set out the rules.

Rule 1: Everything runs on Ether

In this community, there will be no more need for sterling. Any work that's done in your community – supply energy, labour tools – is done on the basis of Ether. You figure that people have phones… and they can exchange the currency easily over a private message group.

Rule 2: No one controls Ether

There will be no central authority controlling Ether. Every transaction that happens in your community will be registered in the private message group for all to see. It will be a complete history of transactions that will never be changed or redacted. You want total transparency. Anyone who wants to check the transactions and the price of Ether could just look it up on their phone.

Rule 3: If you want to participate, you need to stake your Ether

The important thing is that everyone participates. You want everyone to feel like they are a stakeholder in this. Some of the early nomads already place an enormous amount of faith in you. They expect you to be an engineer… a politician… a lawyer. You are constantly settling disputes!

So you have an idea. You will design a system of contracts based on Ether that will automatically settle all transactions. The contracts will be easy to use and will execute automatically once a few simple rules are met.

For example… If the Smith family needs solar power, they can pay 50 Ether to the group and they will receive a metered supply for the month ahead. If the Lynch family needs a blow torch, they pay two Ether and get a deposit of 0.5 Ether back if they return the blowtorch in three hours.

Everything will be self-executing, like a vending machine. And sure enough, your system proves an enormous success. You watch as the system scales in almost no time at all. Soon there are smart contracts for everything: energy, blowtorches, rent, taxes, lending, borrowing. And in this way, you watch as a fully-functioning economy boots up. A system with nobody in control… no banks… no middlemen... an automatic network that thrives with each new family that arrives.

You draw a sketch of how the economy of Nomadland has developed. For a while, it was all centralised around you. Then it started to look like B.

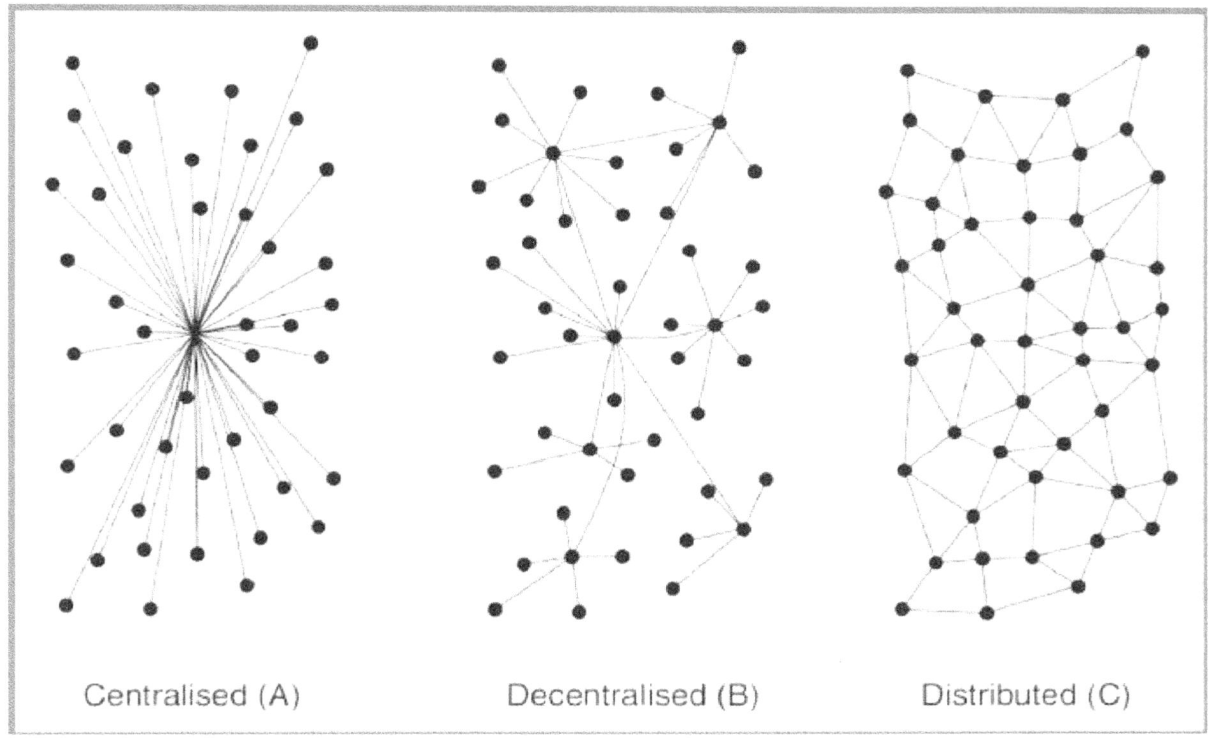

After six months, you have a completely decentralised system where everyone trades with everyone else on the basis of Ether.

The Real Ether is So Much More

This leads me to the real world version of Ethereum because in the last few years something like this story has played out on this platform. A community has sprung up out of nowhere that offers every financial service you could think of: dollars, automatic exchanges, lending, liquidity pools, asset management, risk profile, flash loans. And we think these are the building blocks for a completely new financial system.

The project was started by a Canadian Russian programmer named Vitalik Buterin. There are many strange myths that surround Vitalik. We know he was an extremely gifted child with a natural proclivity for programming, and an ability to add three-digit numbers in his head twice as fast as the average human.

We know he invented Ethereum when he was just 19. He has an unusual appearance, with a voice that sometimes sounds like a synthesiser.

But Vitalik is an amazing spokesman for cryptocurrencies. And the platform he has created truly is a marvel. Vitalik first heard about Bitcoin from his father in 2013. And he was quick to recognise that Bitcoin was going to explode into the mainstream.

Here was a technology that made it possible for anonymous strangers on opposite sides of the planet to exchange value without a bank or government or anyone else in the middle.

That was the beauty of Bitcoin: it was an engine for creating consensus in a group of complete strangers. In the traditional financial system you need a central authority. A central bank to issue currency. A system of commercial banks to issue credit. What Bitcoin proved was that you didn't need any of that. A currency could be created by a community, and sent and received by anyone who chooses to participate.

It was beautiful to see this system scale to the point where millions of people could exchange value without a central authority.

But why stop at just money?

The more Vitalik looked at Bitcoin, the more he recognised that it was just the first in a series of crypto projects that could completely decentralise society. He realised that if he wrote a version of Bitcoin with the right programming language, the network could function like a massive global network where everyone could pitch up and start offering services to complete strangers.

You could replicate Facebook, reassemble the stock market, or even build completely digital corporations and run them beyond the jurisdiction of any government entity.

So Vitalik assembled a team of programmers and they spent almost a year there, hunched over laptops, eating carrots and sleeping on the floor, hatching their plan for a new type of platform that could host their parallel economy.

What we are witnessing is a perfect storm of collapsing trust in the integrity and competence of government, bankers, brokers, lawyers and real estate agents… and the arrival of a technology that is opening the way to the codification of money and trust itself.

How fast will this story happen? It could take a decade. Maybe less. The boom in decentralised finance coins this year gave us a taste of how quickly the Ethereum economy can scale. These are projects that could displace many aspects of traditional finance.

When you combine blockchain technology with traditional money there are all sorts of new ways to establish trust and settle transactions.

Why Investing in Ethereum is Like Investing in Amazon in the Early Days of the Internet

We think billions will be locked into this platform in the coming year. And there are real signs that a new financial system and more is booting up.

Marc Andreessen, who made his money in the early days of the Internet and whose VC fund is going deep on crypto, has caught the mood of the market…

"The payments system we use today was designed more than a half-century ago, and the way we transfer and distribute value has lots of room for improvement. Transferring actual value quickly and cheaply without a third party, in much the same way we currently transfer data like emails or photos, will soon be technologically possible at massive scale.

"Blockchain could be the bedrock of a new system that significantly reduces friction (unnecessary fees, call centres, delays, privacy breaches, and generally antiquated processes) and provides a more modern user experience."

It seems that disruptive technology is coming for finance.

We saw this story play out with retail and distribution. It happened to transport, travel agents and hotels.

All of this is being built on Ethereum! So you see, the big picture fundamentals for Ethereum have never looked better and we see big gains in the medium to long term.

The Key Risks to Investing in Ethereum

Risk 1: Will it Scale?

One legitimate concern is that Ethereum layer 1 is reaching capacity and this will limit growth. In particular the average daily transactions on Ethereum spiked massively during the DeFi boom.

That's why the launch of Ethereum 2.0 is such an important event. Ethereum 2.0 is an upgrade to the Ethereum blockchain. The upgrade aims to enhance the speed, efficiency, and scalability of the Ethereum network so that it can process more transactions and ease bottlenecks. This should tackle the 'capacity' concern.

Then there is the energy problem. The methods for encrypting Bitcoin, for example, require a network of individuals who can 'mine' new coins by computing complex problems. This requires a huge amount of server power.

By one estimate Bitcoin mining consumes as much electricity as Denmark. In terms of energy consumption, Ethereum currently drains about 11.83 TWh every year – that's about as much as Sudan. Ethereum 2.0 will go a long way to solving the energy problem.

Risk 2: Regulation

Then there is the risk of scrutiny by the regulators. The regulators may feel that they need to intervene, and this could cause a few targeted crypto projects to burn up or disappear, which might damage the value of Ethereum holdings.

Risk 3: New Competition

Finally there are a host of new platforms emerging, each with efficient verification methods that could eat into Ethereum's dominant position. We'll look at some of the most promising challengers later in this book. Despite these risks, we are extremely bullish about the long-term potential of

Ethereum.

It has already scaled so quickly. Within another five to 10 years, Ethereum may well have become the basis for a radical reinvention of the entire financial system as math, code and encryption replace human systems of trust.

The implications of this economic warfare are quite staggering when you consider that the economics of the 20th century was predicated on increasing debt as a means of driving growth.

And if you consider that blockchain, Bitcoin and Ethereum have no basis in debt or direct interest payments to central authorities, then we are set for the deepest possible change in our way of life for quite some time.

Chapter 4

Trading the Cycle

In this chapter, we will start by talking about when to enter a market (i.e. buy a coin). We want to focus on the actual nuts and bolts of the top approaches to timing a market entry. These strategies are benchmark traditional finance strategies and they apply to all markets, and we have tailored them to crypto over a period of nearly 10 years.

We have tried out literally hundreds of different entry strategies and back-tested different ideas, and the conclusion we have reached is these are two good strategies for entering a market: Buy the dip. Buy the throwback.

It may appear brief but has been honed and improved over those 10 years.

Cutting out the noise and being focused on a proven approach is how the big money is made. Both strategies are based on charts where the time frame is one day (i.e. each candle equals one day).

It may look easy to do, but having the patience, long-term view, emotional strength and conviction to execute these strategies can be difficult in practice.

Michael's Story

Our lead trader in the Academy, Michael, has been investing in these markets since 2013. It's enabled him to quit the 9-5 and to live in different countries around the world.

That's because all you need is a laptop and an Internet connection. And it's made him the kind of money he'd never dreamed possible. Between 2017 and 2019 alone he made over a 52x return.

He wouldn't tell you this to brag or boast. And we're certainly not suggesting you'll become a millionaire overnight from crypto trading. In Michael's own words: *"The volatility is immense, and we've been through an awful lot of events in recent years, the early days getting in Bitcoin and before it peaked in November 2013, experiencing a long two-year bear on with Bitcoin.*

"And I've been involved in two Ethereum bubbles and have traded well over 100 current cryptocurrencies. I've made thousands and thousands of trades. So I have a lot of experience in crypto. Back in 2013, it was very niche. Now it's exploding. There are new users coming on every day and people are getting more and more interested."

Michael obsesses over charts and price action, and what new coin is going to change the world and what are the real fundamental values and propositions and how the market behaves in cryptocurrencies because it's a very unique market.

He's currently sitting on profits of over 50x over three years. And that's with his risk spread across a number of different assets. He didn't just get lucky with one coin.

Cryptocurrencies offer spectacular volatility and huge increases and huge falls, which is why they are attracting traders and investors from all over the world.

'The key idea to understand is the market cycle and to stay in it for the long term', says Michael.

Some investments grow very slowly.

Others follow a hype cycle, with one big jump in expectations and then a period of disillusionment before the investment finally recovers. That was the story with dotcom stocks, which took nearly a decade to recover from the bubble.

The 4 Phases of a Crypto Cycle

Cryptocurrencies follow a different kind of cycle. They are constantly rising and falling, rising and falling. At the time of writing, there have been six major cycles so far, and these swings can be extreme.

Crypto bull markets go higher than you would expect and bear markets can go lower than you would expect.

There are four general phases in a complete cycle:

1. Accumulation Phase
2. Bull Phase
3. Parabolic Advance Phase (i.e. end of bull phase)
4. Bear Phase

The Bitcoin chart below shows the long cycle from 2013 to the start of 2018.

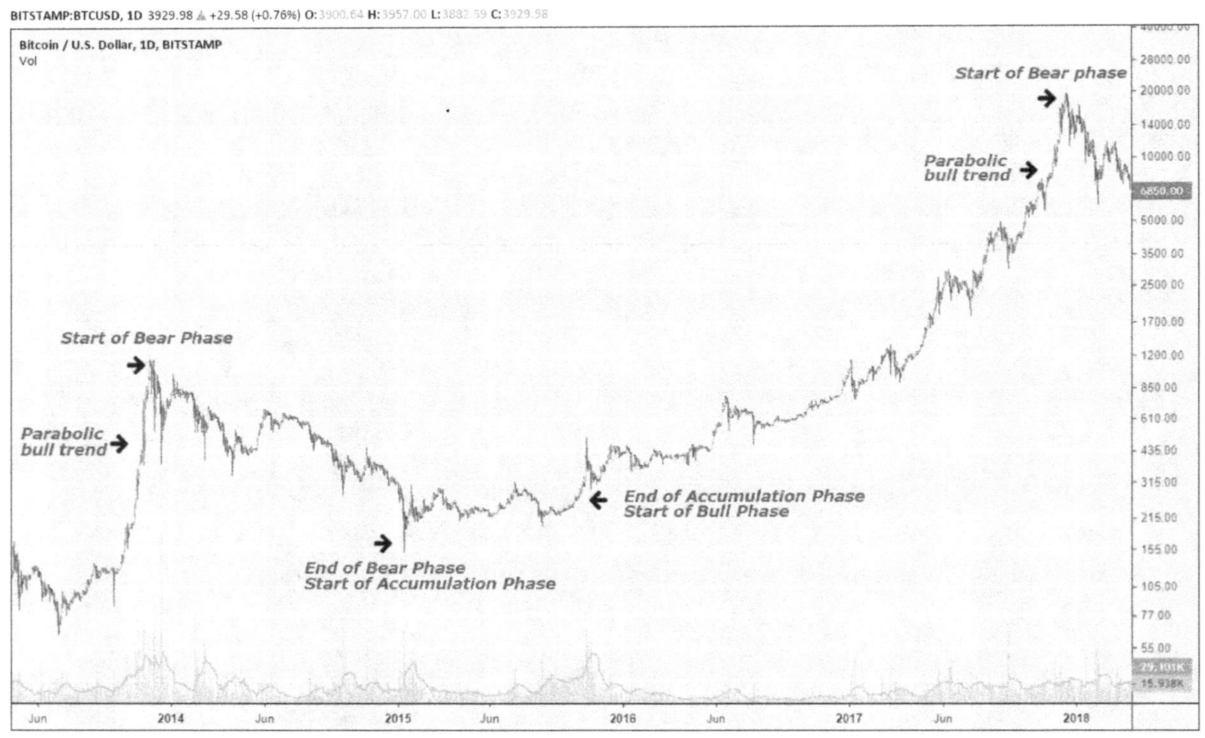

Accumulation Phase

We see the above accumulation phase beginning at the start of 2015. This is when the market bottomed. There was a huge down wave and many of the most inexperienced traders left the market. Articles in the media preached doom and gloom. There are obituaries written for Bitcoin.

It was at this point that smart traders started buying back into the market: just when fear was at its worst. They bought this big dip with the belief in the long-term potential. They accumulated coins for a few months and waited for the market to start climbing again.

It's incredibly hard to time the actual bottom of the market. But by picking up coins during this phase in the cycle, they put themselves in a position to make serious returns.

Bull Phase

After trading sideways for the best part of a year, the market began to pick up again in 2016. This was the start of the bull phase. At this stage, the market had been stable for a while and began to move higher. The early majority were getting on the bandwagon.

The media started to wonder if the worst might be over. And as the appetite for risk returned, the market began to climb very quickly.

As this phase began to mature (in 2017), the late majority jumped in and market volumes exploded. The price of coins soared.

Parabolic Phase

Then the market went a little crazy. The media were now regularly talking about crypto and there were spectacular gains during this period. You've got the example of Ripple between 2015 to 2017. During the 2017 bubble, it increased 55 times against Bitcoin in the space of a few weeks. It was 5,500% up at one point, making it the third biggest market in cryptocurrency.

This is the most enjoyable part of the cycle. It doesn't last long. But if you have put yourself in a position to profit, the gains are outrageous but it's also higher risk as it's closest to the bear market.

Bear Phase

And then it all came tumbling down. The market crashed 60% or 70% or 80% and there were long months of tedium while you sat on your hands, waiting for the market to bottom. Then you start accumulating again. You can trade the down swing in the market. But you'll need a strong stomach for this and we don't recommend this strategy unless you are very experienced.

From start to finish, this cycle can take two or three years. But the time element is notoriously hard to predict and it is only clear that a phase of a cycle has ended when it is clear the next phase is well under way.

For example, the Bitcoin accumulation cycle in 2015 lasted nearly a year (other accumulation cycles have been much shorter) and it was only likely that this accumulation phase in 2015 had ended once we saw a large spike in prices above the accumulation range.

Of course, this appears obvious in hindsight but it can take a lot of skill and stomach for volatility to successfully get in during accumulation!

The most important thing to understand is that the biggest and best gains are made from accumulating coins with sound fundamentals. The better the fundamentals of the coin, the more likely it is to pump and the easier it is to get people on board and drive a mania.

That's an approach that suits a lot of traders and investors. It's all about having a long-term belief and understanding and trying to buy when the market is low.

Three Strategies for Trading Crypto

If you get bored with that strategy, says Michael, if you are looking to trade a bit more actively, or you join during the bull phase of the market then you might consider a few simple buying strategies.

These three strategies work in each stage of the market cycle, however they need to be tweaked depending on what phase of the market cycle we are in.

Approach #1 – Buy the Dip!

The percentages highlighted in this section are applicable first and foremost to Bitcoin and then secondarily to Ethereum.

They also apply to other smaller high-risk coins – or so-called 'alt coins'. The general rule of thumb is that alt coins are more volatile, so dips will be more extreme. The lower the market cap of an alt coin, the more volatile it is.

Bull Phase

In a bull market, buying the dip is simply a good idea! The basic theory is that you have the ideal trading conditions to buy a coin when it's in a bull trend AND when the price is oversold (i.e. a dip).

The simplest and best method is the % dip from the local peak. It cuts through all the noise and encapsulates a lot of complex technical analysis indicators within its simple approach.

Any dip over 20% in a bull market is a good entry for Bitcoin.

Any dip over 30% in a bull market is a great entry for Bitcoin.

The larger the dip, the better the entry but also the lower likelihood of actually making the entry.

This log chart below of BTC vs USD of the 2016-17 bull phase clearly shows all the major dips and their final % retracement size (note: not all 20% dips are shown).

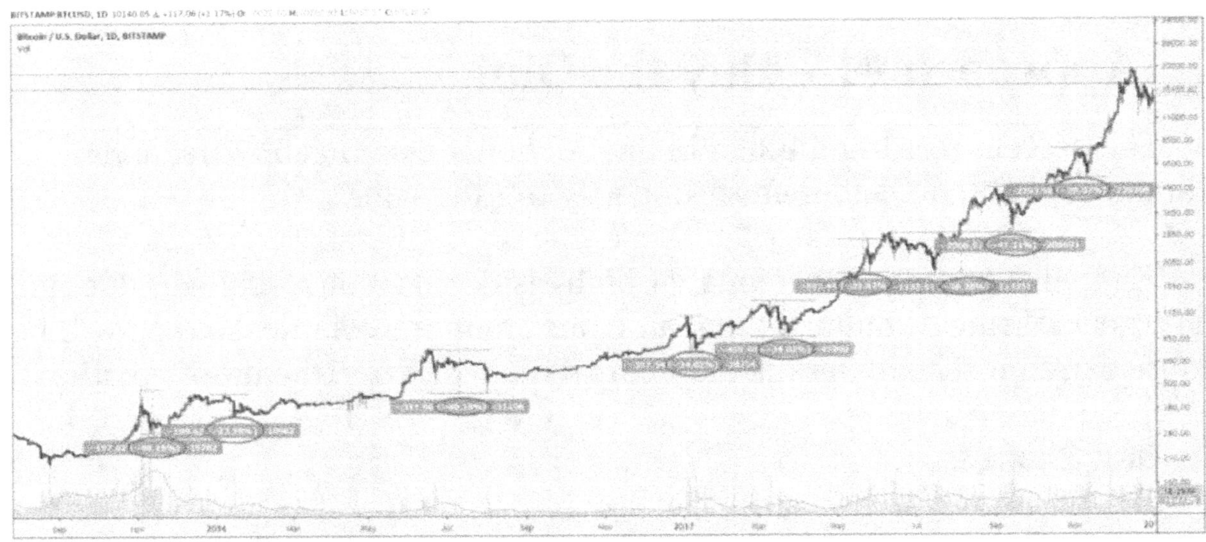

Bear Phase

It is substantially riskier to trade in a confirmed bear market. It's a good idea to trade less in a bear market. You can use stop limit orders to limit the amount you could lose. You also look for deeper dips to time an entry. Over 35% is a good entry and over 50% dip is a great entry.

Accumulation Phase

It is a challenge to know if it is in an accumulation phase or not as it may just be a pause in a bear market, or a bull market may already have started. It is only obvious in hindsight.

In an accumulation phase, you can look to build long-term positions in Bitcoin and Ethereum.

Approach #2 – Buy the Breakout

In this approach, you buy a coin when the price exceeds a previously established peak and key resistance area. This can be found by drawing a horizontal line across significant price peaks. You don't need charting software to do this, you can see it visually or set price alarms to know when a price breaks out.

The coin is to be bought when the price breaks out past the resistance area and preferably when it is a decisive break with good volume. The black lines in the below image highlight resistance lines and subsequent breakouts:

The stronger the daily candle is through the resistance zone, the higher likelihood of a strong price increase.

The typical components of this set up are a peak, then a dip to create the horizontal resistance line. Then just a breakout of this line is required.

This is a great approach to never get left behind in a bull market. The below chart shows a nine-month period during the early stages of the Bitcoin bull run and shows numerous well-established breakout opportunities.

It also nicely highlights a throwback opportunity which we will discuss in the next section.

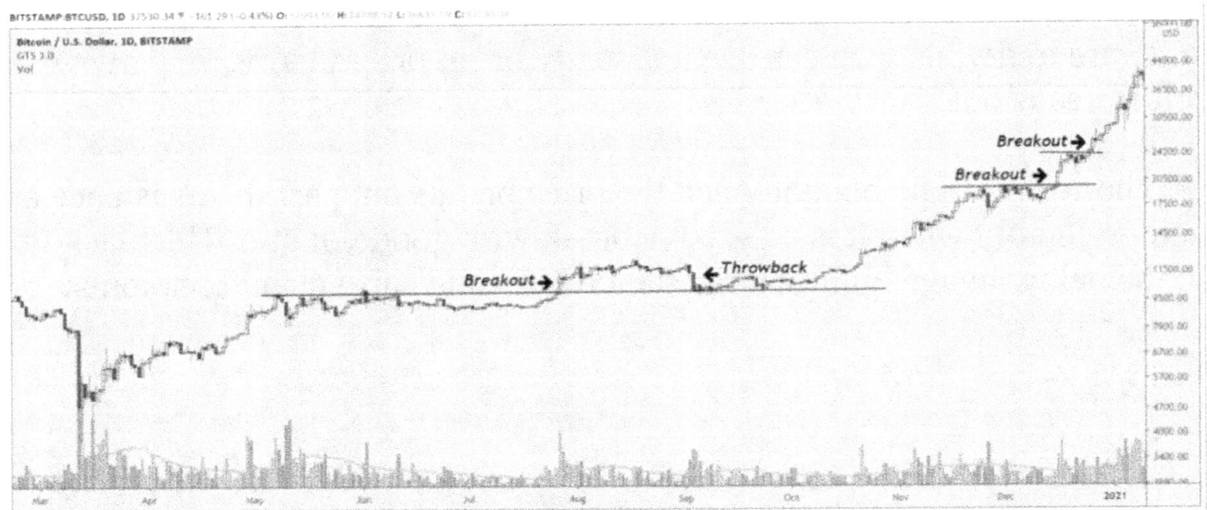

Approach #3 – Buy the Throwback

This is a great set up for an entry that happens very often in crypto.

Essentially, after a breakout occurs (see Approach #2 above) the price often 'throws back' to the original breakout point. This previous resistance zone now becomes support and the price 'bounces' off it before continuing in the direction of the trend.

You would be amazed at how often this happens. However, you cannot always rely on it as a breakout often doesn't throwback and just continues with the trend.

The next chart shows a two-year period in the 2016-17 Bitcoin bull run and, as you can see, there were plenty of opportunities to buy the throwback:

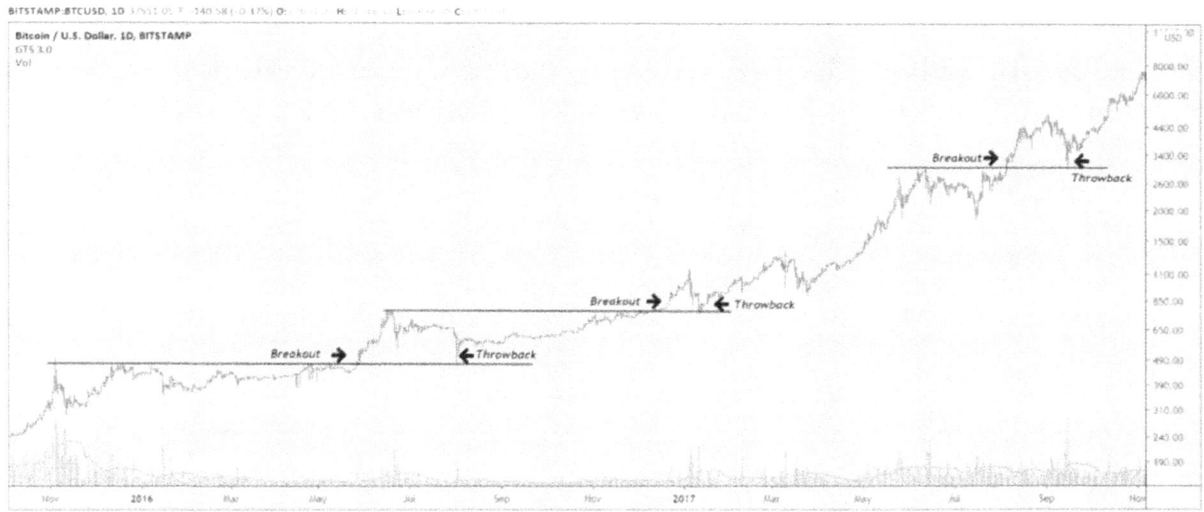

See below for a chart of UNI (a crypto called Uniswap) in a four-month period showing two textbook breakouts followed by two throwbacks:

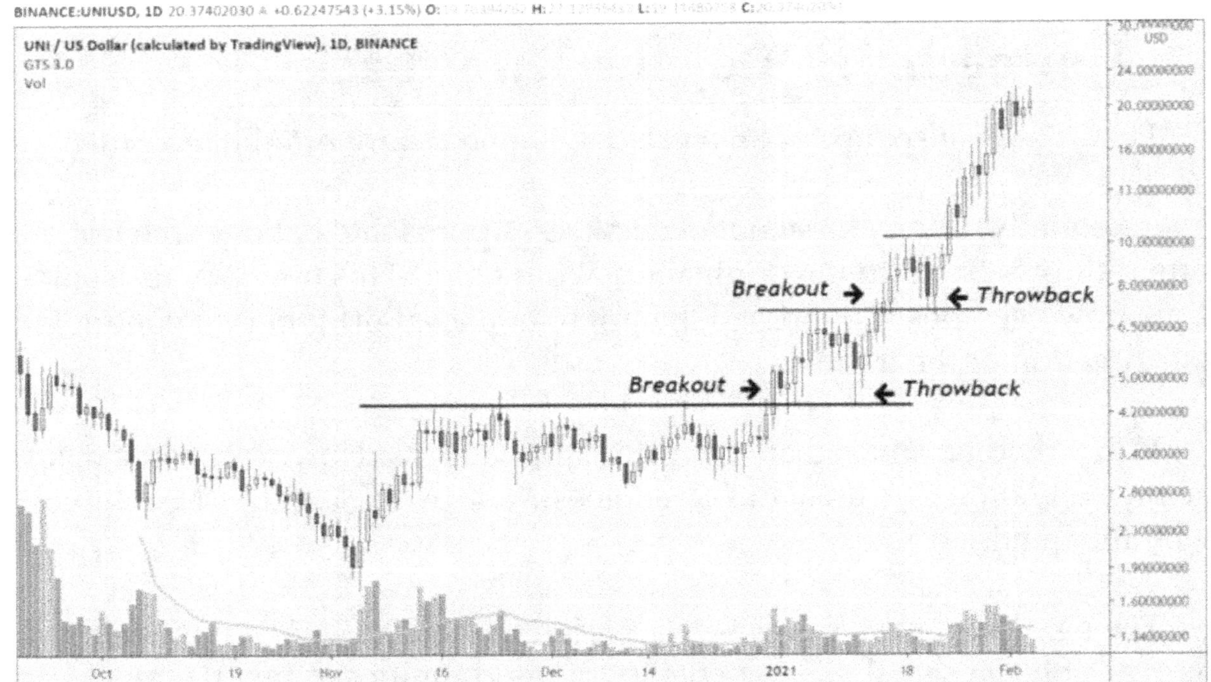

In both examples buying either the breakout or throwback is a great entry. See below for a chart of UMA (a crypto called Universal Market Access) in February 2021 showing a textbook breakout followed by a throwback:

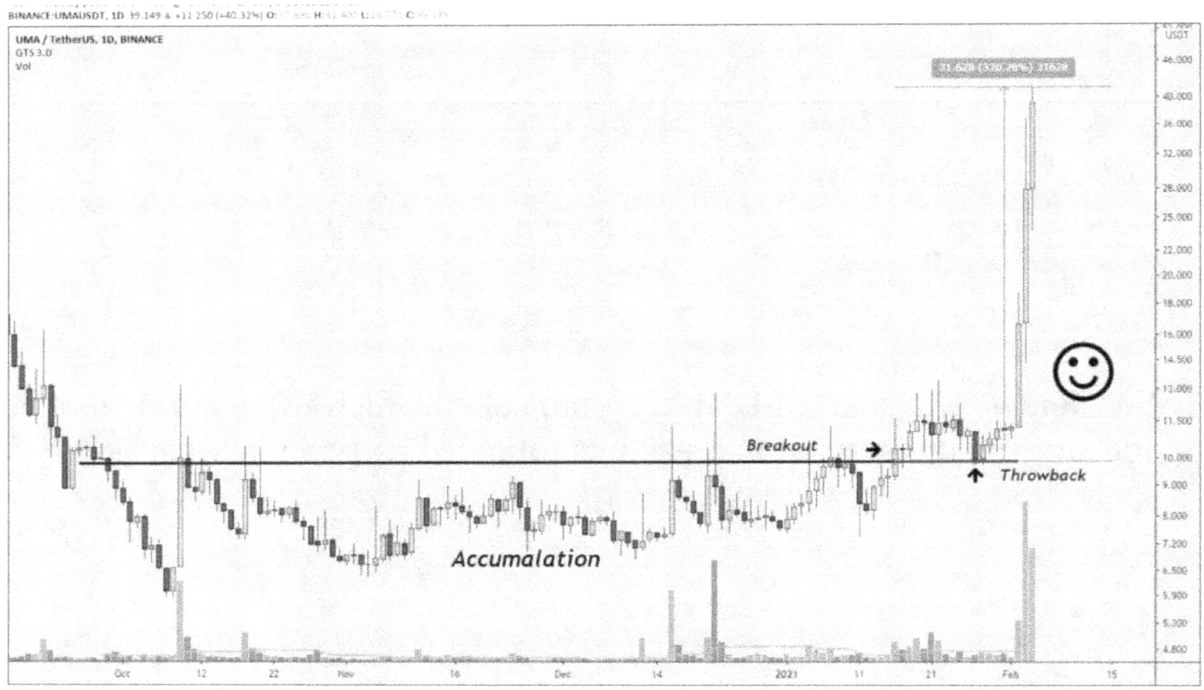

Buying for a Fundamental Reason

Of course, sometimes a coin looks really good from a fundamental perspective and great value at whatever its current price. Fundamental reasons include use case, technology, market, team, some news, landmark event, etc. and I just want to buy in, based on my analysis.

In Summary

Michael trades all three approaches frequently when he enters a market. Although he tries to minimise his trading in general and avoid overtrading. He says he prefers to get into a market at a great time and let his winners run and ride out the bull phase as that's where the enormous gains can be made.

What often happens in practice in a bull market is he will first try and buy the dip. Then if he can't buy the dip for whatever reason (missed the entry, there was no major dip, etc,) he will often try and buy the breakout. Then if he has missed the breakout and there is a throwback he can buy the throwback (if there is one).

In the course of trading, you might experience volatility. That's only natural with this more advanced approach. Here we'll turn to one of our favourite traders, Rich Fitton, who for many years wrote the excellent *Traders' Nest* letter, and his experience of trading a wide variety of markets. His hard-won advice applies just as well to crypto as it does to forex and stocks.

Five Steps to Managing Trading Stress

As traders we deal with external stimuli. That means things that are happening outside your mind and body. And your brain filters each individual 'stimulus' event in two ways… it's seen as either a threatening event or a non-threatening event.

So imagine now logging in to your trading account. You're checking progress on an open trade. Things are going in your favour, the trade has almost reached your target and you move your stop loss to lock-in a good chunk of profit. This is processed as a non-threatening situation and you are rewarded with feelings of calm and well-being. Feel-good chemicals serotonin and dopamine are released into your nervous system.

Now imagine the opposite situation…

You log in to your account and see a load of red numbers.

The trade is moving against you and you see a negative balance in your profit/loss column.

It can be difficult to control your natural response to this type of stimulus. Your brain can process it as a highly-threatening situation (even though on a logical level you know that losses are simply part of the game). Your sympathetic nervous system starts firing up and… now it's crunch time!

Your sympathetic nervous system is what gives you the 'fight or flight' response. It is preparing your body to deal with a real-life physical threat.

Reach the point of it triggering and you risk trashing your carefully-tested strategy in an emotional frenzy. Fighting the market with 'revenge' trades is common here. As is bailing out of the trade 'before things get worse', even though your strategy clearly says you should stay in. Your built-in survival mechanisms actually start to work against you. And this is the exact point at which traders can start to go astray. But there's a small window of opportunity that'll let you control your state of mind before launching into full fight or flight mode. And don't worry if you miss it, there's still something you can do to manage things. Here's how you do it:

1. Spot your incoming stress sign

You just need to start paying attention to recurring physical feelings that let you know your fight or flight mechanism is igniting. It might be a tightness in the throat, tension in the chest, a swirling sensation in the stomach. It's different for everyone. But there will be a sure sign an emotional response is on the way…

2. Put the brakes on now (if possible)

So you've noticed your recurring physical sign. And you can tell your fight or flight mechanism is about to kick in. You now have a very short window of time to acknowledge this is the stage you're at and to break the state. It takes a bit of practice but visualisation and breathing techniques can be used here (you just need to act fast enough). Do the job well and you'll quickly correct your response, stop the full-blown emotional response in its tracks, and be able to carry on business unaffected.

3. Remove the ability to do damage

If you didn't catch things in time at step 2 (and it does take a bit of practice) you'll now need to let the sympathetic nervous response take its course. Your body will flood with fight or flight chemicals and there's little you can do until your nervous system has flushed itself clean.

This doesn't mean it needs to affect your trading decisions though! You simply need to remove yourself from the trading screen for a while (removing the risk of emotional actions damaging the integrity of your strategy). Go for a walk, take it out on a punch bag in the garage, go and chop some logs in the garden.

Just keep yourself out of mischief for about 20 minutes – that's how long it'll take your nervous system to reset itself. A physical activity really does work well if it's possible for you at the time.

4. Analyse what triggers your 'fight or flight' response

So once your nervous system has returned to normal you can start analysing exactly what tends to trigger the fight or flight response in you. It'll be related to fear at some level, and not necessarily a fear of losing money. It can be something more deep-seated like a fear of 'being wrong'. And once you know exactly what you're dealing with you can start to improve things…

5. Practice engineering more appropriate responses

A technique called 'reframing' can be helpful here: Instead of looking at losing trades as an assault on your skills, you can reposition them as investments made in future profits.

This can help neutralise the fear of being wrong. And consider this – it's probably the most useful trading exercise I ever performed…

Aim to take a string of very small DELIBERATE losses in quick succession and then reward yourself for doing so. It can quickly blunt any sensitivity to taking trading losses. Rehearse performing the responses you feel are most appropriate and most helpful – with money at stake for added realism – and you can go on to reap the benefits for years.

There's nothing shameful or negative about experiencing stress when trading, it's how you handle it that makes all the difference!

Chapter 5

Staking

In this chapter, we are going to look at a lower stress approach to profiting from cryptocurrencies. If you are bullish about cryptocurrencies (as you know, we are) and plan to sit on your favourite coins for the long term, then you might want to consider 'staking'.

Staking is one of the most popular ways to earn money in crypto. It can be a fantastic way to grow your long-term holdings without doing any extra 'work'.

In simple terms, when you stake your coins, you set aside a portion of your crypto assets to help support operations on a blockchain network.

Typically, any assets you stake are then locked-in for a fixed period of time: say 30… 60… 90+ days.

And while your coins are locked up, you are rewarded with a high-interest APR as an incentive. It's not quite as safe as keeping your money in a bank. Your capital isn't covered by the Financial Services Compensation Scheme (FSCS), which insures up to £85,000 of deposits in a bank or building society account in the UK. Cryptocurrencies are high-risk assets but the rewards for staking are very attractive.

We have undertaken a comprehensive review of the best ways to stake your coins, and in this chapter we'd like to give a brief overview of our findings.

The best places to stake. The rewards. The risks.

This will help you develop a basic staking strategy, so you can earn a decent return on coins, no matter what stage you are at in the cycle.

Who is Staking For?

In general, staking tends to work best for long-term holds that you have no intention of trading, no matter how much the market fluctuates.

So, for example, if you intend to hold Ethereum for the next 12 months (regardless of whether the price shoots up or down), staking can be a great way to quickly grow your investment.

Ultimately, you can stake Ethereum for a month, two months or 12 months. There are a huge variety of options.

And in return, you earn a decent yield: 5-10%+ depending on the platform.

In general, the main decisions you will have to make are:

1. What coins to stake
2. How long do you want to lock up your coins
3. How much you want to stake
4. What platform you want to use

The super-technical option is to become a full validator on the ETH platform.

You'd need a substantial minimum investment to do this, a ton of technical know-how and a giant computer rig (oh, and your electricity bills will also be HUGE). However, let's put that one aside because there are far simpler ways to stake coins and earn rewards.

We've undertaken a review of each of these and think there are two reasonable options: check out the Resource Guide for the latest information.

Option 1: Stake On an Exchange

This is by far the simplest way to stake your coins. Exchanges such as Kraken, Binance, Coinbase and Crypto.com offer staking. They are very user-friendly, and if you have an account already, then this is probably your best option for getting started.

On Binance, for example, there are a wide range of coins that you can stake. You'll find the staking section under 'Binance Earn' on the homepage.

There are a few different durations – 15, 30, 60 or 90 days. Once staked, you can't withdraw your coins. Binance will hold those coins in a crypto wallet and stake the coins for you.

And at the end of the duration period, your coins will be returned, along with the rewards and interest that you've earned. If you are willing to lock your coins up for 90 days, you'll get a better return than 15 or 30. Some coins are more popular than others and might be sold out.

The pros of using an exchange are:

1. It's very simple
2. You can earn fixed and variable rates
3. It's secure

4. There is very little ongoing effort

Option 2: 'DeFi' Staking

If you are not using an exchange then you might choose to stake coins directly to their own community.

Take the 'DeFi' corner of the crypto market. One of the biggest stories in crypto at the moment is the movement towards Decentralised Finance: a new financial system that is built on Ethereum, which allows people to trade, borrow, lend securely, without the need for middlemen.

This includes: new stock markets and new currencies, new ways of investing.

By staking directly on the staking page of one of these projects you can make serious income, although it comes with higher risk.

And the set up requires the use of MetaMask as an intermediary. MetaMask is a wallet that you can use for holding cryptocurrencies. It's easy to use and you can link it up to a wide variety of websites and apps. You can find out more on how to use MetaMask in our Resource Guide.

You can access it here:

http://thecta.io/resourceguide

The rate of interest oscillates wildly, but here's an example of a DeFi coin where you could earn 34% APR at the time of writing.

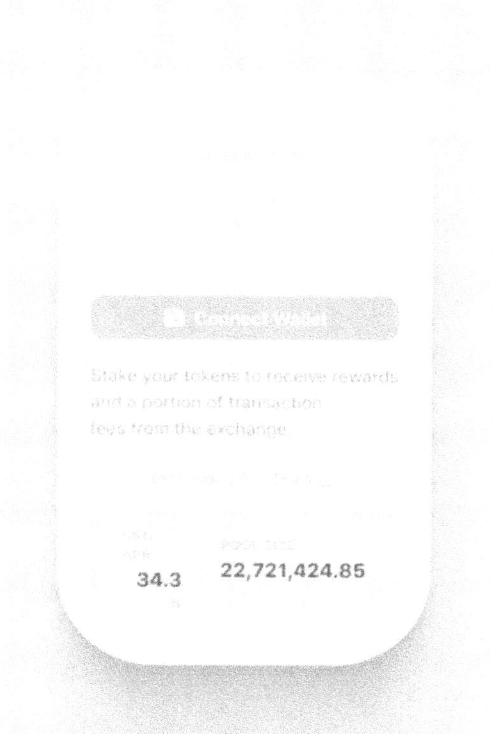

It's a question of connecting your MetaMask wallet to the app. The rewards are handsome, and it's easy to set up.

Unlike the exchanges, there is no lockdown period. You can keep your stake in there as long as you like BUT if you keep it in longer (and don't release your stake early) you can earn additional interest. In this example you can also receive significantly greater gains under what they call their 'vesting' program.

It's worth pointing out once again though: there are risks with any investing and particularly with crypto and some of the smaller projects.

The rewards do vary, and if trading collapses on these platforms then the staking rewards will fall with it. And because you are using your own wallet, you have no recourse in terms of security.

The beauty of crypto is that it's open to all and not controlled by the bank BUT that can also be its downside. At present there is no oversight and you have to take responsibility for the money that you put in this wallet and be responsible for your own security.

What Are the Risks of Staking?

There is the opportunity cost. As you know by now coins can go up (or down) in value several hundred per cent in a matter of weeks.

So if you're an active trader, this is something to consider. If your crypto is locked up in staking you won't be able to (in most cases) release it instantly to make trades. For most people it makes sense to stake with a % of your portfolio rather than with everything at once so that you are diversifying your portfolio and spreading your risk.

Other risks around staking include the regulatory risk, which it's worth keeping an eye on.

Once again our most trusted exchanges are Kraken and Coinbase. MetaMask uses sound technology but, again, you have no recourse if you lose your logins or if something goes wrong.

In Summary

There are some great returns to be made from staking, as long as you're comfortable with the risk.

It can also be a good way to keep yourself motivated and on course, mentally.

When there's a burst of relentless gains, crypto is easy. Everything is positive and exciting… the six and seven-figure gains suddenly seem in reach… but even just a few weeks or months of sideways markets and dips can be hard, boring, frustrating… emotionally draining.

Having some of your long-term assets working for you while we weather the storm and wait for the markets to bounce back can be a great focus (not to mention profitable!).

As you'll discover, there are a multitude of other ways to earn income from your cryptocurrencies too.

How Long do I Have to 'Lock In' My Crypto When I Stake?

It completely depends on the program. Most staking programs are now very flexible (but do always check the terms). There are flexible plans (0 days lock-in)… 30 days… 60 days… 90 days +.

Also it's worth bearing in mind that on the majority of exchange staking programs (Ethereum and a handful of others being notable exceptions) you can still 'unstake' and withdraw your crypto even when you're locked in. This normally takes around 24 hours to process. In most cases you will lose any interest you accrued but that's all.

Others are flexible staking plans with no locked-in period whatsoever. You trade as much as you like while still accumulating rewards (though the interest is lower).

What is the Safest Way to Stake?

Staking always involves some level of risk, however, long-running Exchanges with a greater level of regulation likely offer the lowest level of risk. You have a customer service contact if something goes wrong (which doesn't exist with something like MetaMask) and in general there tend to be far greater levels of flexibility should you change your mind.

They also offer the lowest barrier to entry.

There are no gas fees (we'll cover these in more detail a bit later) or complicated set up.

The downside is that in some cases they will offer a lower % rate (in some cases significantly so).

Which is the Most Profitable Staking Platform?

It depends on the program but in general going direct (no middleman!) is the most profitable method.

Sometimes this is a mind-bogglingly difficult process and fraught with risk (we don't recommend these methods) but other programs are very straightforward.

When you stake your crypto directly with a project you tend to get the highest rates. If you have long-term confidence in a particular coin this is often the best bet. However, as ever there are pros and cons to this. A lot can happen in the crypto space and projects may get usurped over the long term. Calculate whether the time/cost is worth it for the reward gained.

How to Stake Your Crypto on Kraken

Staking your crypto on Kraken is one of THE easiest methods out there. (As you'll see it only takes a minute or two!). There are a few different ways you can stake on their platform – as they make their staking option available on most pages – but all offer the same outcome.

What follows is the simplest step-by-step approach.

You can see all of the different coins you can stake in one place and they display all the risks and rewards in one easy-to-read table:

Step 1: Login to Kraken

You can do that here:
www.kraken.com

Step 2: Head over to the staking page

Now head over to Kraken's dedicated staking page here:
Kraken's Staking Page

Here is what you'll see on this page:

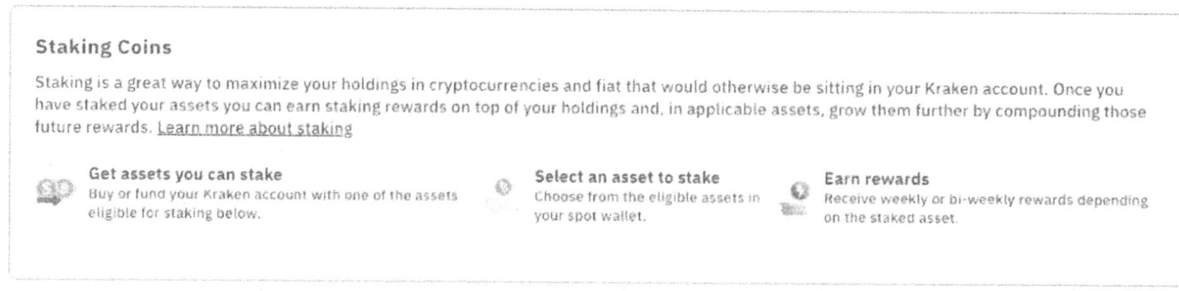

Staking Coins

Staking is a great way to maximize your holdings in cryptocurrencies and fiat that would otherwise be sitting in your Kraken account. Once you have staked your assets you can earn staking rewards on top of your holdings and, in applicable assets, grow them further by compounding those future rewards. Learn more about staking

Get assets you can stake
Buy or fund your Kraken account with one of the assets eligible for staking below.

Select an asset to stake
Choose from the eligible assets in your spot wallet.

Earn rewards
Receive weekly or bi-weekly rewards depending on the staked asset.

STAKING BALANCE	£0.00	TOTAL REWARDS	£0.00

Staking assets Stake Unstake

Asset		Reward rate	Total rewards	Staking balance	VALUE (GBP)	Actions
Polkadot	DOT	12.00%	0.00000000 DOT	0.00000000 DOT	£0.00	
Kusama	KSM	12.00%	0.00000000 KSM	0.00000000 KSM	£0.00	
Kava	KAVA	20.00%	0.000000 KAVA	0.000000 KAVA	£0.00	
Cosmos	ATOM	7.00%	0.000000 ATOM	0.000000 ATOM	£0.00	
Tezos	XTZ	5.50%	0.000000 XTZ	0.000000 XTZ	£0.00	
Flow Hold	FLOW	4.60%	0.00000000 FLOW	0.00000000 FLOW	£0.00	
Flow	FLOW	4.60%	0.00000000 FLOW	0.00000000 FLOW	£0.00	
Ethereum	ETH	5-7%	0.00000000000 ETH	0.00000000000 ETH	£0.00	
Cardano	ADA	4-6%	0.000000 ADA	0.000000 ADA	£0.00	
Solana	SOL	6.5%	0.00000000 SOL	0.00000000 SOL	£0.00	

*Reward rates reflect the annual percentage rate (APR). All reward rates are estimates subject to change and compliance with Kraken's terms and conditions.

Learn more about staking

Neither your Kraken account nor staked assets are covered by insurance against losses or subject to Federal Deposit Insurance Corporation (FDIC) or Securities Investor Protection Corporation (SIPC) protections. For more information, please see our Terms of Service.

It's worth taking the time to read all the text they provide on the page (always check the latest live version) as it runs through the rewards and risks involved.

On the left-hand side you can see the name of the cryptocurrencies that Kraken currently offer staking on. To the right of this is the estimated earnings reward as a % and this is calculated as APR (or an annualised rate). Bear in mind that these annualised rates are just a guide. The rate for many of these coins will be variable and as such liable to change.

Step 3: Check over the terms and place your stake

Now it is simply a case of clicking on the little staking icon next to the coin you wish to stake (as pictured below). A little pop-up screen will appear that confirms your estimated reward payout, intervals and so on. Make sure you read, understand and are happy with everything on this screen before proceeding.

If you are happy to proceed, you just need to enter the number of coins you wish to lock into staking in the box at the top (it can be a decimal if you like, e.g. 0.5) then click 'Continue'.

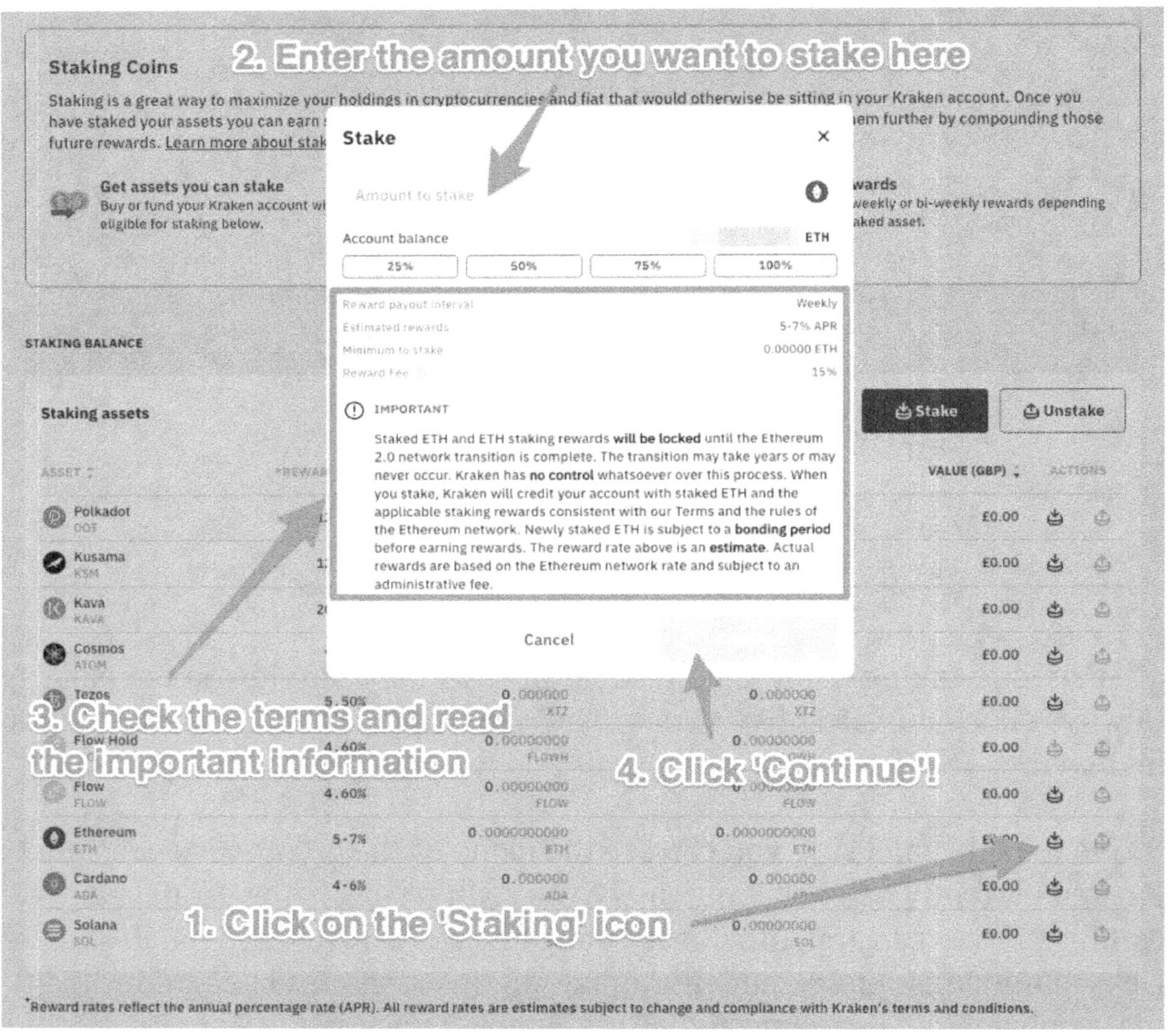

Please note: we've just used Ethereum as an example here and you may well get better rates elsewhere (and/or the option of not being locked-in for such a long period).

Step 4:

At the time of writing there is one last pop-up screen just ensuring that you understand the terms and are happy to proceed.

Please bear in mind that the information displayed here will vary according to which coin you wish to stake.

If you are happy with everything, type 'I accept' into the box as instructed and then click 'Confirm', and that's it!

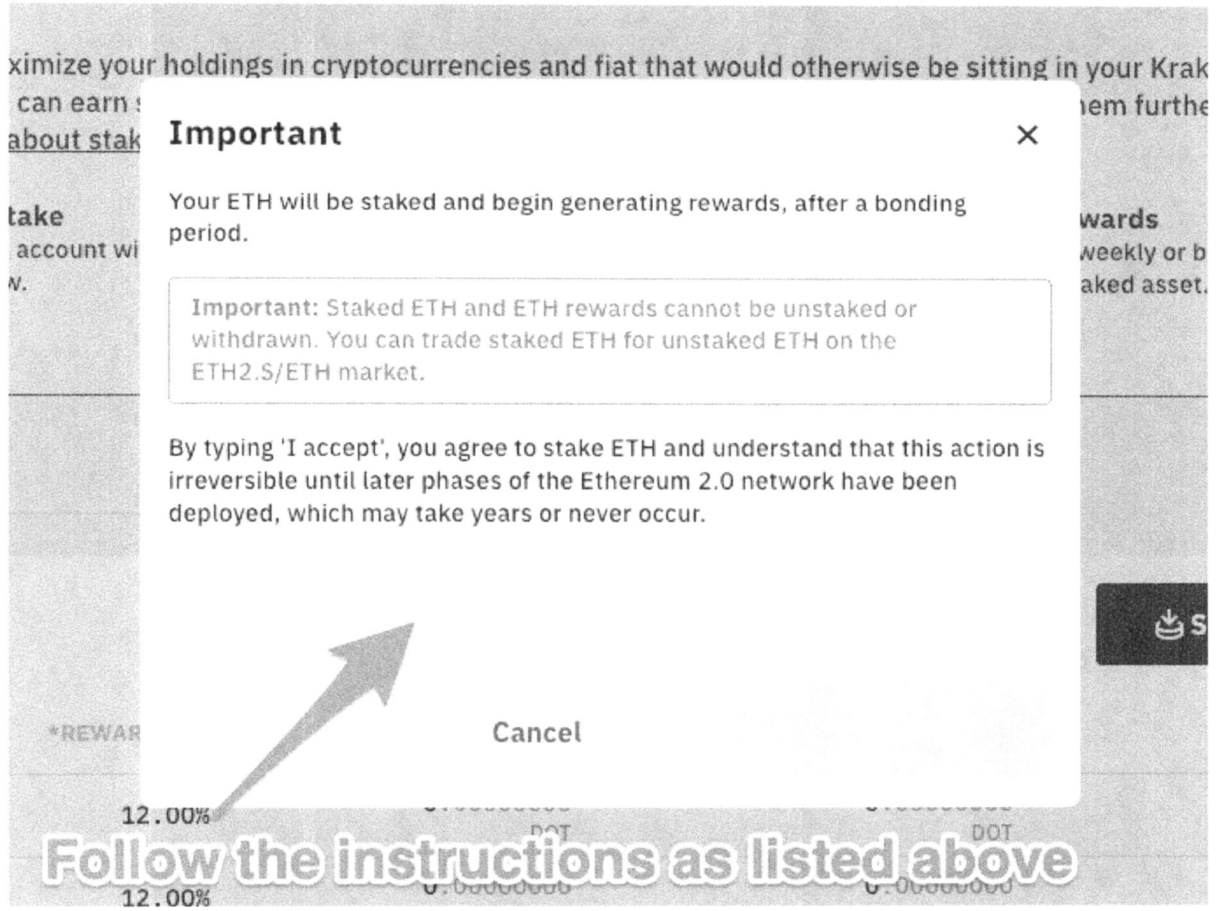

Step 5: Check back to monitor your rewards

If you want to check back, see how your staking is going (and monitor your rewards) you can do so simply by clicking back on the staking page at any time:

Kraken's Staking Page

From here you can also choose to 'Unstake' any coins where available.

Please note: For some coins, like Ethereum, 'Unstaking' won't be possible until the transition to ETH 2.0 has been completed. While this transition is proceeding well there is no fixed date as to when this might complete (or indeed guarantee that it will do so).

That's why it's important to properly read through the terms and make sure you are happy with the risks involved. Other coins may offer more flexible staking programs.

That's it!

Kraken is one of the oldest exchanges and has a great track record. In terms of ease and stability there is a strong option for staking particularly for long term holders.

Chapter 6

AirDrops

AirDrops can be another fantastic way to increase your crypto profits *even* further.

It's a way of receiving free crypto that's sometimes worth 3, 4 or even 5 figures.

In this chapter on AirDrops we're going to look at:

- What are AirDrops?
- Why on earth are they giving away free money?
- A brief history of token launches
- How to best position yourself for an AirDrop

What is an AirDrop?

AirDrops are where you're gifted completely free crypto by certain (usually new) projects in the crypto space in return for using or interacting with their app or platform.

Uniswap is a great example. In 2018 Uniswap was a successful crypto project that people were actively using. However it was token-less. This meant that investors couldn't trade 'Uniswap' as an asset in its own right on crypto exchanges.

(Think of Facebook before their IPO. They already had a HUGE and active userbase for several years (2004-2012). Yet ordinary people couldn't invest until they launched on the stock market and became tradeable in 2012. Shares are very different to tokens but you get the idea.)

In 2020 Uniswap launched their own token, UNI. To reward early adopters they 'AirDropped' a share of their tokens to their users. They gave 400 UNI tokens, for free, to every person who had made a transaction using their platform before a certain date (17/10/20).

Today that 'free' money is now worth many times that original stake. And that's for doing virtually nothing! All they had to do was place a trade they were going to make anyway using their platform.

Why on Earth Are They Giving Away Free Money?

There are four main reasons AirDrops are popular with developers.

1. It *increases* the decentralisation of the project (i.e. It pulls us away from the current set up, whereby 'centralised' individual companies control/manipulate ALL the flow of data).
2. The possibility of an AirDrop encourages people to use their platform or app, it effectively bootstraps a new network.
3. It can massively help raise their profile.
4. It doesn't cost them a penny to do so.
5. It helps with regulators if you give the tokens away for free, it's not a security sale.

You have to remember that crypto is a wildly competitive space changing at breakneck speed.

There are literally THOUSANDS of different projects all competing to be *the new Internet… the next form of currency… the trading exchange that everyone wants to use…* you name it. The opportunity is so enormous, people are flooding in from 'traditional' tech and finance.

Some of these developers believe their ideas are genuinely revolutionary (and many are) and want to get as many users on board as possible to show them.

As more people hear about it and use it you create a network effect and the numbers swell.

One of the best ways they believe they can do this is to gift people who use their platform with a load of free crypto (of their particular token).

It's an effective strategy for the aforementioned reasons and people love free stuff (particularly free money!), and it's a win-win for everyone involved. If it gets people using and adopting their apps and platforms, the developers are happy. If users get a share of their token as a thank you, they're happy too.

It also helps get around some of the legal wrangles by making the project more decentralised.

How to Best Position Yourself for an AirDrop

As we've just discussed, AirDrops are gifted to early adopters of certain apps or platforms.

Crucially apps or platforms that don't currently have their own token.

So we need to do two things:

1. Find promising crypto projects that currently don't have a token.
2. Start using their apps or platforms.

That's the core of it. We then just need a little lady luck and hope that they launch their own token. If they do, and if we took the right action using their platform (by placing a trade on it or creating a wallet or whatever the criteria is they decided on), then we could be in for a big payday.

And here's where it gets really exciting… sometimes you can get *multiples* of this, depending on the AirDrop and the circumstances.

For example, some AirDrops will pay out the same amount to *every single wallet you create and use* with their platform. Remember, these wallets are free to set up and there are no limits to how many you create.

In a bull market, with projects that have real use and value, some of these AirDrops can be worth huge sums of money, and as a strategy AirDrop hunting can be used in tandem with your mainstay crypto investing.

By the way, there is an emerging platform Michael has spotted, where simply staking can qualify you for multiple free airdrops, at the current rate it's about 2-3 per month. This is the most straightforward way to position yourself for AirDrops. You can find out more in the Resource Guide.

You can access it here:

http://thecta.io/resourceguide

AirDrops: Pros, Cons and Caveats

The number one thing to bear in mind is this: we can't control whether any of these projects will launch their own token or not.

There will be some that do but also many that don't. It's down to the individuals behind each project and their timelines and ideas. And while some will launch a token… it might be several months or even years down the line, so patience is needed.

So there are three things to be aware of:

1. There is always uncertainty – you can't guarantee you'll receive an AirDrop for the reasons listed above – However, you can dramatically increase your chances.
2. It's sometimes a bit of a faff. You're following guides and setting up wallets here… and making transfers there, and doing this there and that and it can be fiddly. It's not difficult, just a bit of a pain. It all depends how deep you want to go. In cases where you want to use that app anyway, it's no work at all. The ratio of work to reward will for many people, make this a no-brainer because some of the rewards are staggeringly high and could be worth £6,000… £10,000+ for minimal work.
3. You may end up spending some crypto on gas fees – when you make swaps, transactions or movements between wallets there's usually a gas fee, which is a charge for the work needed for that transaction to take place. Gas fees vary hugely per platform and will eventually come down as the technology evolves, but can be quite high at present particularly on Ethereum. These charges are dropping all the time BUT they are relevant and you need to bear this in mind. That's why in general we'll recommend an approach where you use these for transactions you want to make anyway, even if you weren't looking for AirDrops.

It's important to factor all this in because it's not just a case of do this, then that, and you're guaranteed to receive an AirDrop…

But there is one core fact.

Use some of these platforms and apps and you're in with a great chance of landing a big payout or multiple smaller payouts.

And we're genuinely talking thousands and even tens of thousands of pounds in some cases here.

Don't and your chances are ZERO. It's also an incredible way to understand some of these projects, to get to grips with the technology and to really be out there on the cutting edge.

And that's not just nice to have. This has real utility. Some of these apps will introduce you to ways of trading lesser-known coins that you can't find on traditional exchanges.

You'll also have new ways to trade crypto at drastically lower gas fees.

And right now, while there is huge competition and a frantic race for market dominance from new apps and platforms, there couldn't be a better time to get involved. Most ordinary people are still pretty clueless about crypto, let alone AirDrops, which makes the profit potential disproportionately high right now.

Chapter 7

The Growth Mindset

In this chapter, we've got something a little bit different for you.

We want to talk about something that we think is one of the top priorities for any trader: the concept of a growth mindset.

Now, you might have heard this in many different contexts, it's applicable to almost any form, any aspect of your life. From relationships all the way to your job or any endeavour you choose to take on.

We think this is a game-changing way of looking at things, particularly in trading and investing and particularly in crypto, because it's such a minefield and a graveyard of people who couldn't handle the pressure.

Here is how our lead trader, Michael, has developed this mindset over years of trading crypto.

Developing a Growth Mindset

"If I look back over my last eight plus years of trading and investing in crypto and other investments before that, the number one mistake that I see, and I've seen it literally hundreds if not thousands of times, is people give up. They get disheartened in a bear market. They lose 80% from the peak to trough and decide to give up. They don't understand why it happened to them.

The pressure in their mind is too much for them to take. And you can have a lot of sympathy for that because I find trading and investing very difficult at times.

To a large extent, that's what I like about it, it's hard. I have tried to not work and to do a semi-retirement and I'll be honest, it's boring. I came back with a renewed vigour to do things that are difficult, to constantly grow, regardless of my financial situation. I try to always look to be moving forward and growing. And that's what led me to this idea of a growth mindset.

It's based on a book by Dr. Carol Dweck. It was written back in the noughties. Bill Gates credits it, as he says on the cover: "The value of this book extends way beyond the world of education. It's just as relevant for business people who want to cultivate talent and for parents who want to raise their kids to thrive on challenges."

So, it's applicable to basically everything, and it's extremely critical to crypto. In fact, I distilled the core concepts of the entire book down into a table for you:

No.	Area	Fixed	Growth
1	Abilities & Work	Innate & unchangeable	Improve through focus and practice
2	Failure	View failures as permanent	View failure as a chance to learn and improve/pivot
3	Critical Feedback	View as personal attack	View as a chance to improve
4	Task Selection	Choose easier tasks Put in minimal effort	Embrace challenging tasks Work hard to improve
5	Ability to finish difficult tasks when faced with obstacles	Give up when faced with an obstacle	View obstacles as a chance to experiment and learn by solving new problems
6	External Validation	Focus on measurable accomplishments	Focus on continual improvement
7	Risks & being courageous	Less likely to take risks or face our fears	Embrace risks as a way to innovate & improve
8	Other people's success	Is intimidated / jealous and feels like a failure relative to the successful person	Is inspired by other people's success

This is how I see it. I prefer small, simple, clear points, but this is my own summary that I wrote on the book.

What I'm trying to do is build this concept to use on a long-term basis and really integrate it into my whole way of thinking and behaving in life and as a trader.

Two Avatars

So how does it work? Well, according to Dweck, there are two types of people. There are some people who have a bit of a growth mindset, and some people who have a bit of a fixed mindset.

It doesn't matter which mindset you have now. The whole point of undertaking a growth mindset approach is you're going to look to move towards reaching a growth mindset.

Let's look at each of these eight points and see how they can be approached differently with a fixed and a growth mindset.

You Can Always Improve

A fixed mindset person typically thinks that their abilities are fixed, they're innate or unchangeable. While a person with a growth mindset thinks you can improve your focus and practice.

Now I see this all the time, amateur traders and investors love to look at something and exclaim, "Oh, I just get it". Or perhaps they were good at maths at school or studied economics at university, or they have 15 years' experience trading. They're a natural.

There will always be an element of natural ability but, fundamentally, it's completely demonstrable and true that you can improve your focus and practice. So, you need to shift your mindset to think, I can always improve and by the application of hard work and focused practice, I can get better. And over the long term with this attitude, you will compound on that effort.

I think that every bit of time you spend in crypto and learning about the markets, learning about the technology, that's all compounding your experience. The newbies from the latest cycle, will be more experienced for the next one.

Failing is Healthy

So a fixed mindset really sees failures as a kind of scar or an X on their track record. There's some part of them that thinks they are innately bad. But fundamentally, when you fail, it's a chance to learn and improve, or pivot, or change. All the greatest titans in business have had huge failures. Many of them have gone bankrupt or lost it all more than once.

Failing is a part of life, and it's about not letting those failures get you down or stop you from getting back up. With a growth mindset attitude you need to dust yourself off and think, "Right, I've gone through this failure but it's not going to have a serious long-term impact in my life. I know, if anything, what not to do."

What can I do differently? How can I improve? And I think that's a really important lesson.

In our crypto trading we will all pick coins because we think we know what will happen and then the price will go the wrong way or we will just get it wrong. That will happen. It will happen multiple times.

It's not about beating yourself up, it's about learning from that failure and then looking to improve.

Attitude to Feedback

Point number three, is critical feedback. A fixed mindset person views that as a personal attack. They immediately drown out any of the content of what's said, and all they feel is disrespect and attacked. They get defensive and wound up and they get cranky and annoyed.

Whereas a growth mindset person listens to the feedback, asks questions. They seek feedback in the first place and use that feedback to look to improve and move forward and get better.

And it's not easy to do. None of these things are easy to do. And again, we know about them all kind of intuitively but I think seeing them spelt out and reminding yourself of this is quite important.

Do Hard Things

And the next point is task selection. A fixed mindset person typically chooses easier tasks and puts in minimal effort. They'd rather be a big fish in a small pond. They look around them and they compare themselves to others and they try to put themselves beside people where they know they will win and be relatively good.

They care about what other people think, and they pick easy things so that they can get some wins. Meanwhile, a growth mindset embraces challenging tasks and works on really hard tasks to improve and always looks to get better.

And these kinds of areas overlap. If you're not afraid of critical feedback, if you're not afraid of failing, if you're very comfortable with applying yourself and working hard, then it makes it easier to choose hard tasks.

Even choosing to get involved in crypto is a difficult task. The amount of people I know who told me in 2013, they missed the boat, and in 2014, in the bear market, they just decided: "Oh, that's not for me."

And this will continue, and they'll just never get involved. Because the truth of the matter is they just don't want to embrace something that's difficult and challenging. And because they can't handle the concept of risk, the idea of failing, putting money in and losing some even if it means making more. And so they choose things within their circle of confidence, and they don't embrace the difficult task.

Finishing a Task

The next point is the ability to finish difficult tasks when faced with obstacles.

A growth mindset will view obstacles as a chance to experiment and learn by solving new problems. I mean, this is crypto all over.

Crypto is still on a daily basis, for me, about trying to get my head around exactly what's happening. There's so much to learn, so much to take in, so much technical stuff, fundamental stuff, emotional stuff, trading aspects, the investing side of things, long term, short term, medium term. The wider economy and technology is endless. It really is. And a lot of people just think it's too much for them.

Even the simple task of setting up an exchange account. We have seen this time and time and time again at Crypto Traders' Academy. People join the group, and they go to set up their accounts. Then they can't get set up for whatever reason. They don't try to set up several exchange accounts. They don't put the time and effort in and they give up when it's hard.

However, those with a growth mindset will see these challenges and think: "OK, it's hard to set up an account right now but that means other people find it hard. OK, that gives me a bit of an edge. Now I've learnt this step I found hard, what's next? What will I learn next?"

You Don't Need Validation

Some fixed mindset people focus on measurable accomplishments. They like things like degrees or job titles or salary levels. Whereas a growth mindset person doesn't really care as much about what other people think. They don't look for badges or certificates. What they want to do is improve. And you know yourself whether you're improving or not, regardless of what sticker, badge or certificate you get.

And I think that is so important in crypto because it doesn't matter if you joined the race yesterday. This isn't going anywhere for 10, 20, 30 years. There's so much to learn. And in six or seven years' time, people will be talking about you being an original investor with loads of experience.

But that's only if you focus on continually improving and moving forward and increasing your skill set.

Taking Some Risks

The next point is taking risks and being courageous. Fixed mindsets are less likely to take risks or face their fears. Growth mindset people embrace risks as a way to innovate and improve. That is one of the hardest parts of crypto because it's so risky. It's so volatile and you can lose your shirt. But it can also make hundreds, thousands, hundreds of thousands, millions of shirts as well.

You have to embrace that risk. You have to realise that without any risk, there's no reward. And whenever you're doing something that's particularly risky, I'm not saying, "be stupid", but embrace the risk in a measured, smart way and learn how to innovate and manage that risk and improve.

A lot of people can't handle risk. They can't handle difficult things. There's a difference between people who succeed in entrepreneurship and those who don't, which is very similar to trading and investing.

The difference between entrepreneurship and having a salaried job is risk, and you're living at risk every day. It's about embracing that risk and seeing it as it is.

Don't Worry About Other People's Success

The last point here is other people's success. In a fixed mindset, people are intimidated and jealous and feel like a failure relative to a successful person, whereas a growth mindset person is inspired by other people's success.

And over the course of my life, that's one I have needed to work a lot on. I've always looked at the people around me. I've always intuitively tried to surround myself with super-high performers, both in my education and my personal life. I've always been drawn to some crazy, crazy, clever people who work hard and are interesting. And yes, it's sometimes got me down when other people are successful and I'm not. And now some people might look at me and say, they feel the same way about me!

But what I do know is that if you surround yourself by other people who are very successful and have a lot to give, you can learn and be inspired by them. You need to be inspired by that success rather than being intimidated or jealous.

And that's another one of the keys to success in this space. If someone makes £10 million, £20 million or £100 million out of this, the key is not to think, "Oh, if only that was me." Instead think, "How did they do it? What can I learn? How can I get myself there eventually?"

In Summary

And so that's the eight areas. I work on these points on a regular basis. But just being aware of these things and applying them to your crypto investing and trading and realising that you know this is hard and you will fail sometimes, that you will have hard things to choose, is part of building a growth mindset.

I really believe having a growth mindset is important to how you live your life and to be successful at crypto trading and investing.

Having been in eight years of bull and bear markets, I know when you've only been in it for a year or two, you tend to focus on the next week or month ahead, but by stepping back, taking in the big picture, you are already adopting a growth mindset.

And if you apply this framework over the long term and you compound it, you're going to be successful. I believe it applies to everything: physical health, mental health, your learning, your career, raising kids, relationships and anything else."

Chapter 8

Your Next Steps

We're so glad you decided to learn more about investing in cryptocurrencies. We know you will be very keen to dive in and get started.

We recommend starting small. Crypto trading can be quite a ride, with markets rising and falling more in a day than most markets would do in a week. While that's one of the reasons why this market is so exciting, it's also the thing that catches many newbies out.

They pile in with a big chunk of their bank, then get panicked by the volatility and they end up selling out for a loss. This is a huge shame as it often means that they give up at the first hurdle.

We know it is hard to stay calm when things fluctuate so wildly but my suggestion is that you start small.

Use a stake that won't worry you if the price takes a sudden dip. If you are just starting out, we suggest something between £500 and £1,000 as a good place to start. Then you can scale in with more money once you're comfortable with the volatility. And of course, never risk any more than you are prepared to lose. That's the most important point in this book.

That way you won't panic sell and make a mistake. You can sit back and ride out the ups and downs.

Another tip that might give you peace of mind: when you start making gains, take out your original stake so you are just using your profits to trade.

Get Some Skin in the Game

After that, it's a question of getting fully involved. If you have made it this far then you have everything you need to buy Bitcoin or Ethereum.

So get going. Get some skin in the game. This has the potential to be a huge story in your life; a way to make life-changing returns.

We've already helped others make five, six even seven-figure returns from these markets and would love to help you too.

Bitcoin

Bitcoin is a digital form of money.

It allows people to send or receive money securely over the Internet, even to someone they don't know or trust.

The total supply of Bitcoins is capped at 21 million, so, like gold, it has a finite supply.

What sets Bitcoin apart is that it's decentralised, meaning there is no single point of failure, there's nobody in control of it who can tamper with or forge it.

It's the first decentralised peer-to-peer payment network that is powered by its users with no central authority or middlemen.

Just like the pound, dollar or euro you can:

- Send it from one person to another
- Trade it
- Hold onto it as an asset (like gold)
- Use it to pay for goods/services

Blockchain

The blockchain is the engine that powers Bitcoin (and the crypto world).

How Does it Work?

Here's where it gets a little more complicated… The blockchain is a peer-to-peer network of users – people like you and me. Every participant remains anonymous at all times.

It has, in-built, a clever system of checks and balances in-built to ensure there's no foul play. In other words, everyone using the network participates and keeps the system running, but no one can control or influence it.

This means that Bitcoin and the blockchain cannot be taken down or destroyed and it means every transaction is logged and verifiable.

Buy Order

A buy order is an instruction you place on an online exchange (such as Kraken) to buy crypto for you automatically when it reaches a certain price.

For example, let's say Bitcoin is currently priced at around £10,000 but you don't want to buy it for that because you're waiting for it to dip.

You could place a buy order on Kraken to purchase 0.5 Bitcoin when the price drops to £9,500. That way if the price drops while you're asleep, or if you're away from your computer, you can still buy at the price you want.

Coinbase

Coinbase is one of the largest Bitcoin exchanges and currently serves 32 countries. As well as Bitcoin, users can also buy and sell Ethereum and Litecoin. Bitstamp and Coinbase are currently the only exchanges in the UK that accepts debit cards or credit cards as payment.

Decentralised Finance (DeFi)

The biggest story in crypto at the moment is movement towards Decentralised Finance: a new financial system that is built on Ethereum, which allows people to trade, borrow and lend securely, without the need for middlemen.

This includes:

Decentralized exchanges (DEXs): Online exchanges help users exchange currencies for other currencies, whether US dollars for Bitcoin or Ether.

Stablecoins: A cryptocurrency that is tied to an asset outside of cryptocurrency (the dollar or pound, for example) to stabilise the price. This is an easy-to-trade and transfer currency that provides all the speed and efficiency of a cryptocurrency, without the volatility that often comes with crypto.

Lending platforms: These platforms use smart contracts to replace intermediaries such as banks. A huge spike in lending this year has kicked off a craze in 'yield farming', with investors lending their money on platforms such as SushiSwap and Yearn Finance in order to earn huge income payments.

Ethereum

Ethereum is a crypto that was co-created by Vitalik Buterin and launched in July 2015. It's an open-source blockchain-based platform that introduces something called smart contract functionality.

This is heralded by many as a revolutionary breakthrough because it:

- Allows for blocks to be created much faster than they are with Bitcoin
- It means that applications (not just currency) can run on the network. For example, files on cloud-based storage on a decentralised version of something akin to Dropbox. Several new app-based cryptos are being developed that run on the Ethereum blockchain (platform)

Fiat

This means traditional state currency, such as the pound, dollar, euro, etc. For example, you could say: "I'm withdrawing some of my Bitcoin into fiat" (this means I'm selling my Bitcoin and transferring it to pounds/dollars/euros).

Fork

A fork happens when a group of developers decide to take the source code from one piece of software (such as Bitcoin for example) and then create a completely new and independent software development from it. You then end up with two separate pieces of software, the original one and the new version. A fork (or split) like this happened in the Bitcoin community on 1st August 2017 and we ended up with:

1. Bitcoin
2. Bitcoin cash

The reasons for a fork can be varied (such as the desire to speed up transaction times or tweak functionality). Because projects like Bitcoin are completely open source, forks can take place without breaching any copyright law. However, the success of a fork (for the new software at least) will be dependent on how widely it is adopted.

Hodl

Hodl simply means 'hold', as in "I'm holding Bitcoin" (or rather "I'm hodling Bitcoin!"). The misspelling caught on thanks to an early meme in the cryptocurrency community and is frequently used in forums, Facebook groups and reddit threads.

Kraken

Kraken is a Bitcoin and crypto exchange that's the preferred choice by many professional traders due to the lower transaction and trading fees. You can buy a number of cryptos on Kraken including Ethereum, Uniswap, Yearn Finance and more.

Mining

When someone mines Bitcoin they do two things. They help verify other Bitcoin transactions and also release Bitcoin into circulation. This is how the blockchain works and it keeps transactions secure and reliable. Miners are rewarded for verifying transactions which keeps the system running.

What Are They Mining Exactly?

The process of mining Bitcoin involves solving a computational problem. This allows them to chain together blocks of transactions. In return they receive transaction fees and newly-created Bitcoins.

In the early days of Bitcoin anyone could mine using a simple PC from home, however as the network grew and more Bitcoin was mined, the algorithms became more complex and the process more costly.

The cost of the electricity alone means it's not worthwhile for most people and is best left to those with professional (and expensive!) set ups.

Proof of Work (PoW)

Proof of Work is a measure that's put in place to stop system abuses taking place when an individual or party uses a service provider. For example, it could be used to stop spammers flooding email providers, or to stop hackers trying to take websites offline using DDoS attacks.

How Does it Work?

It requires some 'work' from the party requesting a service before granting them access. This work needs to be difficult (but possible) from the requester's side but easy to confirm on the side of the service provider.

This is known as the CPU cost function. In simple terms, it's designed so that the amount of work needed to try and get past/overwhelm/break the Proof of Work system in place is so immense as to make it virtually impossible.

Proof of Work is used in Bitcoin mining to ensure that transactions are correctly approved.

Private Key

A private key is a bit like your pin number or password. When you open a wallet, you will be given a private key which allows you to spend Bitcoin or crypto or send it to others.

It's extremely important to keep this safe (and ideally kept offline somewhere secure) because if someone steals it they can access and/or spend your crypto.

Satoshi

A Satoshi is currently the smallest fraction of a Bitcoin that can be sent. It is a hundredth of a millionth of a Bitcoin (or 0.00000001 BTC).

Smart Contracts

Smart contracts allow people to exchange items of value (such as money, property or shares) without the use of a middleman.

For example, banks act as middlemen when we exchange money. Solicitors, estate agents and banks act as middlemen when we exchange property. Brokers act as middlemen when we exchange shares.

Smart contracts could remove the need for any of these. They were first conceptualised in 1994 by legal scholar and cryptographer Nick Szabo. In 2015 Vitalik Buterin used blockchain technology (the technology behind Bitcoin) to turn this into a workable protocol. This is called Ethereum.

Tokens

The term token causes a lot of confusion in the crypto space because it can refer to a number of different things, Such as:

- A type of currency used between people (e.g. Bitcoin)
- A digital asset or right (ownership of a thing)
- A stake or share in a startup (for example, if you got involved in the Ethereum token sale)

And those are just three definitions (there are more!). Some people use the word token to describe non-currency cryptos that use the Ethereum platform (as opposed to currencies and coins like Bitcoin). This is because Ethereum generates tokens rather than coins, so this is perhaps the clearest use. However, the reality is that many people use the term 'token' interchangeably, so context is important.

Wallet

A wallet is a piece of software that you can use to send and receive Bitcoin and cypto, a bit like online banking. An example of a wallet you can use for Bitcion is Electrum.